D0276906

Keith Miller

A Cricketing Biography

Keith Miller

A Cricketing Biography

MIHIR BOSE

London
GEORGE ALLEN & UNWIN
Boston   Sydney

First published in Great Britain in 1980

This book is copyright under the Berne Convention. All rights are reserved. Apart from any fair dealing for the purpose of private study, research, criticism or review, as permitted under the Copyright Act, 1956, no part of this publication may be reproduced, stored in a retrieval system, or transmitted, in any form or by any means, electronic, electrical, chemical, mechanical, optical, photocopying, recording or otherwise, without the prior permission of the copyright owner. Enquiries should be sent to the publishers at the undermentioned address:

GEORGE ALLEN & UNWIN LTD
40 Museum Street, London, WC1A 1LU

© Mihir Bose 1979

British Library Cataloguing in Publication Data

Bose, Mihir
    Keith Miller.
    1. Miller, Keith 2. Cricketers – Australia – Biography
    3. Sportswriters – Australia – Biography.
    796.358'092'4   GV915.M/   79-40773

    ISBN 0-04-920062-3

Typeset in 12 on 13 point Bembo by V & M Graphics Ltd, Aylesbury, Bucks.
and printed in Hong Kong.

To Wendy
for everything

Contents

Plates
(between pages 80 and 81)

Acknowledgements

A great many people both in England and in Australia helped me in the writing of this book.

They include Trevor Bailey, Brian Johnston, Tony Pawson, John Woodcock, Brian Scovell, J. M. Kilburn, Jean Bowler, R. J. Cochrane of the Elsternwick Cricket Club, E. T. Clifford, Officer in Charge of Records of the Australian Department of Defence (Air Office), J. C. Elden, Registrar of the Melbourne High School Old Boys' Association, Anne Lamming of the Melbourne High School, A. R. Barnes, Secretary of the Australian Cricket Board, D. L. Phillips of the BBC Written Archives Centre, Stephen Green, the Curator at Lord's, George Stirling of the Melbourne High School, Godfrey Evans, Alex Bannister, Peter Smith, Pat Landsberg, Keith Hebb, a boyhood friend of the Millers in Sunshine, Heck Oakley, Jules Feldman of the St Kilda Football Club, Doug Wright, J. G. Dewes, Rex Alston, Sir Len Hutton, Gubby Allen, Alan Ross, Norman Yardley and F. R. Brown.

To three of them I owe special thanks. While he was alive, Sir Neville Cardus was a constant source of encouragement; in death, he has continued to be a fountainhead of inspiration. Basil Easterbrook was as generous in sharing his thoughts as he is in dispensing his drinks or lending his rich collection of books. And of course, Wendy Wimbush, who read through the entire typescript, suggested unarguable alterations, corrected many errors and helped to put the book together.

Wisden, as usual, provided irrefutable facts and figures. I would like to express my thanks to the following authors and publishers for permission to use material from their books:

Macdonald & Jane's for extracts from *Cricket Crossfire* and *Cricket from the Grandstand* by Keith Miller.

Pelham Books for extracts from *Cricket: The Great All-rounders* edited by John Arlott.

Frederick Muller for extracts from *Round The Wicket* by Bill Edrich and *Spinning Round The World* by Jim Laker.

George G. Harrap for extracts from *Australian Batsmen* and *The Fight For The Ashes 1950-51* by A. G. Moyes.

William Collins Sons & Company for extracts from *Brightly Fades The Don, The Ashes Crown The Year, The Greatest Test Of All* and *Fingleton On Cricket* all by Jack Fingleton; and *From The Boundary* by Ray Robinson.

I would also like to thank Donald Charlesworth, whose ability to read my handwriting is a minor miracle and whose typing is very nearly another, Rose Streatfeild, who has heroically suffered the birth pangs of this book, Mark Streatfeild, who rescued the manuscript between the Grand Hotel, Calcutta, and Dum Dum Airport, and John Newth, who gave it a home.

Without the help of these people the book would not have been the same, though they are not responsible for my opinions or for any errors or omissions.

London
Winter 1979

Foreword

by FRED TRUEMAN

Keith Ross Miller will go down in the history of Test cricket as one of the great all-rounders of all time. In my opinion he will also remain the biggest enigma that Australian cricket has ever produced or is likely to. He had the flair, as any cricketer of the highest class must have, to be able to perform great feats that surpass even one's own expectations. He also had a great personality that influenced all who came into contact with him and I do not think that anyone could say they knew how he would react to a situation on a cricket field. That was where his greatness lay.

When he was bowling it could have been an edged shot or something that a player said or a remark from the crowd that would suddenly change his mood. Or it could even have been an important horse race on television that he had an interest in. Suddenly a wicket that had appeared docile and in the batsman's favour would seemingly change into twenty-two yards of sheer devil-ridden hell. The ball, which had hardly reached the wicket-keeper's ankles the over before, would start coming into the 'keeper's gloves at chest height. The batsman playing and missing as the ball started moving would cause the slips to retreat backwards two or three yards. Miller's influence had to be seen to be believed.

That was the magic of Miller. He had the ability to change the whole course of a match in two or three overs and the crowd would be stunned as the tranquil atmosphere suddenly became one of breath-held tension which you could cut with a knife.

He did not always rely on his pace to get wickets as David Sheppard, now the Bishop of Liverpool, will tell you. In a match at Lord's, just before the close of play, he bowled a googly with the new ball and had Sheppard out lbw. Even the

Reverend David looked to the heavens for some guidance!

That was not the only time it happened. I understand from that great Australian captain and my personal friend, Richie Benaud, that Miller did it again in the West Indies to another Test player. In 1955 when Australia were touring the West Indies they were playing in Georgetown, British Guyana. Keith had had his usual large amount of sleep, which was not easy in the air-conditioned but steamy hotel, before racing up in the first over and bowling a bouncer. Next ball he delivered the 'wrong-un' and Bruce Pairaudeau played at it three times and was out suffering the same fate as the Rev. David.

Miller could incense a crowd with something he had done and with one flash of genius that is the hallmark of a great player would pull something out of the bag and have the crowd purring its pleasure. I remember at the Oval in a Test Match watching Miller standing at first slip as the great Ray Lindwall, his partner in fast-bowling 'crime', was running up to bowl. Miller's arms were folded and he appeared to be looking at the crowd and not taking any interest. Lindwall delivered the ball and the next moment Miller was flat on the floor, facing down the wicket, with arms crossed in front of his face holding a magnificent catch in one hand. I'm still trying to work out how he got there!

Miller's explosive batting could also win a match. He believed in hitting a ball and entertaining the crowd even if the conditions were against him. He could hit sixes with ease and grace and I recall that in 1953 at Kingston in Surrey, after England had won the Ashes, I was one of his victims. I was playing for the Combined Services against the Australians when Miller was dropped at leg slip before he had scored and he took full advantage to make 262 not out. He destroyed me. I failed to take a wicket in 14 overs and conceded 95 runs as Miller produced as fine a display of aggressive, controlled batting anyone would want to see.

When characters like Miller are around there are always the inevitable stories to go with them and there is no shortage when you talk about him. Peter Philpott, the leg spinner from New South Wales, tells the lovely story of when he played his first match for the State side in 1954 against South Australia. NSW had batted and made 270 before the umpires upheld a light appeal which incensed Miller. The next day he was supposed to pick up Philpott on his way to the ground and completely forgot about him! Miller suddenly remembered, jumped into his car, and roared back to the arranged spot. Somehow he made it back to the Sydney Cricket Ground just as the umpires were going out. With shirt flapping and boot laces undone he arrived on the field for the first over and proceeded to bowl South Australia out for 27.

Harris, the South Australian opening bat, finishes the story by saying: 'Yes, I remember because I bagged a pair before lunch.'

But Miller's exploits don't end there, of course. He was made captain of NSW in place of Arthur Morris, who was a fine skipper but deposed because the selectors did not like a captain wearing suede shoes. On one occasion when Miller was leading the team onto the field, Bill Watson, who made a century for NSW in 1954 against the MCC and Frank Tyson, said: 'Hey, Nugget, we have twelve players on the field.' Miller, without turning his head, said: 'One of you b— off and the rest scatter!' That symbolises his approach to the game.

I have my own memories of him. When I bowled him out at Lord's in the 1956 Test match he saluted me by saying: 'You will do for me.' I have never forgotten that tribute.

His human touch was also reflected in the long-running television programme, 'This is Your life'. Before the end of the programme Miller was almost reduced to tears when his family and friends from all over the world paid tribute to him. For me it was proof that he is a sincere and honest man with a heart of gold. That is probably why they call him Nugget. He is a man I've been proud to acknowledge as a friend through the golden years.

1

In the summer of 1974 Gary Sobers retired. That evening I broadcast a tribute to him. On the way home I shared the staff car with a colleague of mine from the news department.

'Gary Sobers?' She shrugged her shoulders. 'I don't watch cricket nowadays,' she said.

'Yes,' I said, 'there is far too much' . . . slow over rate, dearth of class players . . . I got ready to launch my thesis.

Her intervention was decisive. 'Ever since Keith Miller retired. I used to rush to Lord's whenever I heard he was playing'.

My colleague was pretty, vivacious, possibly thirtyish. Miller last played a Test match in England in 1956. I made a quick calculation. She must have been a schoolgirl – and a fairly young one at that – when Miller was in his prime. 'Yes,' and there was a defiant, memory-recalling firmness in her voice, 'he was a treat'.

And as the station played my tribute to Gary Sobers, I felt crushed. Gary Sobers is the greatest all-rounder in the history of the game – there is no serious dispute about that in the cricket world; I did not credit my friend with a great deal of cricket knowledge. But what I had thought was a good broadcast was turning out to be words, mere words: they did not stand a chance against primitive passion. The rest of our journey was completed in absolute silence.

As I write I can understand that passion. Gary Sobers was undoubtedly technically superior but Miller remains one of the most exciting cricketers of the post-war years, possibly even within living memory. Few have commanded such a broad-based following. None has matched the wider appeal that sustained this following, an appeal that was founded on an appreciation of the many faces he presented to his public: the cricketer, the man, the Australian.

Miller the cricketer is in the records. In 55 Test matches he scored 2,958 runs and took 170 wickets. In Australian Test cricket only twelve batsmen scored more runs and five bowlers took more wickets. In the history of the game only the all-round figures of Richie Benaud, Wilfred Rhodes, Gary Sobers and Trevor Bailey stand comparison. Miller in fewer Tests has better figures than either Rhodes or Bailey; Benaud in eight more Tests is ahead in wickets but behind in runs. Only Sobers, over a considerably more congested career, has both scored more runs and taken more wickets. In only two out of his eleven major series did Miller fail to play a match-winning rôle in at least one Test. Even then, in four Tests of those two series he created probable match-winning positions.

Impressive as these figures are, they do not tell of the runs he inspired or the wickets he helped his partners take or the influence he exercised over his contemporaries. For that we must look to the man.

Miller's career straddled the closing years of the Age of Bradman and the opening years of the Age of Professionalism. He was easily the most distinctive cricketer of either age: to neither did he really belong. The Age of Bradman distrusted him because he refused to harness his undoubted gifts for the cause: ruthless, mammoth run-getting in the pursuit of total victory. The Age of Professionalism feared him because it could not always curb those gifts.

And he always sought to do just enough. The decisive intervention: a regal 50, a couple of quick wickets or a marvellous catch in the slips. As a general rule he never lusted after unnecessary runs or superfluous wickets. This is where his greatness lies. He was able to maintain his poise – his highly individualistic approach – over such a contrasting span of time.

William Hazlitt has defined the use of the term 'great' when applied to physical performers:

A great chess player is not a great man, for he leaves the world as he has found it. No act terminating in itself constitutes greatness. This will apply to all displays of power or trials of skill which are confined to the momentary, individual effort and construct no permanent image or trophy of themselves without them.

Remove Miller from the score card and he still lives. That can be said of few cricketers and in the post-war era of only two others – Fred Trueman and Tony Greig. Perhaps a gesture – tossing a bail to the Lord's crowd as he led the victorious Australians off the field in 1956 – or a mannerism – throwing back his hair as he went to his bowling mark – or even a supreme act of athleticism like losing a ball in the middle of his run-up and then like a rodeo performer harnessing an unruly horse flicking it from foot to hand without disturbing his motion. Crowd involvement is an essential part of the Miller story. Miller was always able to provoke a crowd; he occasionally angered them; he sometimes saddened them; he never bored them.

This rapport was fuelled by two of the essential characteristics of the man: his unerring sense of occasion, and his presence.

The Lord's Test is the high point of the English season and it creates a resonance in the furthest corner of the cricket world. Miller never failed in a Test match at Lord's. In successive Tests at Lord's (including the matches of the 1945 Victory Series) Miller made 105 and 1, 7 and 71 not out, 118 and 35 not out, 4 and 74, 25 and 109, and 28 and 30 when he also took ten for 172.

Miller's 'presence' bears the testimony of such a remarkably catholic cricket congregation that only the hardened sceptic will question it. I shall content myself with one witness.

On a mild winter day in late February of 1975 I met Sir Neville Cardus to talk about Keith Miller. We had a leisurely lunch at his regular haunt – the London Steak House – strolled over to his nearby flat in Baker Street, and as the afternoon turned to evening he relived his favourite Miller moments. Cardus was committed about Miller: he believed in his genius, understood his mood. Miller was not one of the 'Welfare State' cricketers he detested: 'Once I was at Lord's; suddenly Arthur Mailey turned up. He had just returned from China, he said. If tomorrow Keith turns up and says he has just got back from the moon, I will not be surprised.'

We discussed many aspects of Miller's career and as we parted Cardus spontaneously offered to write a preface for my book; we arranged to meet again. Exactly a week later I turned to my favourite early-morning radio programme, Radio 4's 'Today'. It was one of the first items in the news: Sir Neville Cardus was dead. The preface was never written.

Miller the Australian completed the image, particularly for the ladies. Physically he looked every inch the ideal type: the perpetual sun tan; the dark and, for the period, longish hair; the blue eyes; the tall, well-proportioned frame – narrow at the waist but broad where it mattered – and, above all, a colonial. Sentiment reinforced libido.

Miller played, and still plays, the part of the colonial to perfection: the visits to Ascot, friendship with famous personalities, guest of the Royals. Godfrey Evans, a close friend of Miller since his playing days, feels that Miller is much more flamboyant in England:

> The social life in Australia is so different. There he is a family man. He likes to spend time with his wife and children. Perhaps a few beers, a swim. And in Australia it is not that easy to gamble. But here he can go to the Royal Boxes, he has many friends in the world of racing, Scobie Breasley gives him a lot of tips.

There is one curiosity. The public Miller is debonair, carefree; the private Miller provokes a strong, protective loyalty. It was the common refrain of his friends as I searched their memories. What are you going to write about him? Do present all the facts. It was as if they were protecting a vulnerable, delicate child.

In the Age of Austerity, Miller was a throwback to an earlier time: the quintessential romantic rebel. It is not that he had elaborate theories about the game or that he wanted to revolutionise its basic structure but that his appeal was essentially romantic and his make-up ideally suited to express a natural, spontaneous rebellion.

Cricket is a finely structured game. It respects order yet tolerates protest. Miller – a six-hitting batsman, a fast bowler – had just the right combination to express, in wholly cricket terms, violence and defiance. A six is at once a measure of a batsman's command – albeit momentary – and an act of defiance. A great fast bowler in action is one of the truly memorable sights of the game: it may prove crucial, it is invariably violent. Both acts provide decisive and often rebellious moments in a game of many nuances and unresolved moods.

But even when Miller rebelled in terms that went beyond the game, as in his disagreements with Bradman, his personal charm prevented any nastiness. What in others would have appeared clumsy or potentially destructive, or both, was in Miller so evidently part of his personality. He was often controversial, never notorious. This, then, is a biographical study of a cricketer and a man, a supreme individualist.

2

Benjamin Street is the oldest street in Sunshine, a suburb of Melbourne. No. 29 is one of a group of four terraced houses – the only ones of their kind in Melbourne – which the locals still refer to as 'English' houses: single-fronted with rooms on either side of a long passage that runs the length of the house. It was here, on 28 November 1919, that Keith Ross Miller was born, the third son and fourth child of Leslie Miller.

It was in some ways appropriate that Miller should have been born in Melbourne (later Sydneysiders would claim him as if by right, with Sir Neville Cardus enthusiastically advertising their claim). Melbourne was the only Australian city to develop under private auspices, its origins were attended by vigorous disputes and it refused to entertain convicts. Something of this fierce independence of spirit and a desire to look to higher things was always part of the Millers. Even as Miller was born, the Smith brothers – Keith and Ross – were pioneering air travel between England and Australia and providing the Sunshine Millers with a name for their child.

Sunshine then, as now, housed a working-class community. Today it is a bustling industrial city peopled with Greeks, Italians and other Southern European immigrants. In the 1920s it had just become a separate borough – three years before Miller was born – and it had a more traditional Australian setting: a community of less than 1,000 people, 400 houses scattered over five square miles, dusty roads and a single factory – H. V. Mackay's Farm Implements Machinery Company – which employed practically everybody including Leslie Miller.

Life in Sunshine was fairly hard. Most of the houses had to rely on tanks for their water supply, there was night soil collection till 1925-6 and neither cars nor wireless. The surrounding plain was barren, and there was a small, muddy creek called Kororoit which also served as the local swimming bath. Seven and a half miles and an indifferent steam train away, Melbourne was a different world: the cinema boom was just starting and the dance halls promised excitement and fun. But the return journey from Melbourne was difficult: the railway ended half-way and the dances and other amusements at Braybook School – a 2½-mile walk – were more popular.

But there were compensations. There were films at the Mechanics Institute, simple and delightful games like quoits at which the Millers became quite proficient (a circular knotted rope was thrown from a distance of twelve feet on to a peg over a foot high and to score the highest quoit one had to reach 100 wins), the one boarding-house in town had a large billiards room which was deservedly popular, and the community was well fed, well clothed, closely knit and contented.

The family was steeped in cricket. Both Miller's older brothers were to become fairly good club cricketers, both Les and Ray being considered better than Keith at one stage. And Father Leslie knew enough about the game to teach his son the rudiments. The education began early. When, at the age of five, Miller was hit while practising with a normal-sized ball, his father decided that a soft ball was the answer. So Miller learned the basics of batting with a tennis ball. This was an important factor. Young boys are notoriously afraid of being hit by a hard ball, and many an unconscious move to square-leg has developed out of childish fears. Miller had no hesitation in getting right behind the line of the ball, his timing developed and his footwork was democratically licensed, always in the right direction: forward to meet the ball rather than in retreat.

It was about this time that the Millers moved from Sunshine to Elsternwick, a neighbouring suburb. This was a more mixed, if older, area: working class co-existed with middle class, labourers lived next door to doctors. Miller started his schooling career here at Elsternwick State School and found the playing fields attached to the school – a rarity in such State schools – a useful and happy training ground.

In this growing industrial suburb Miller developed his cricket. He used a lamp-post as his wicket and when the roads were not particularly welcome there was always the backyard. Miller would stuff a stocking with a ball and measure his strokes against the swing of the stocking on the clothes line.

Playing cricket under such conditions had its problems: dodging traffic, losing balls into the backyards of neighbours – one of whom developed an uncanny knack of anticipating the intruding hit. And benefits: Miller acquired judgement and developed a fierce but balanced competitive spirit. Years later he was to recall the influence of those years. In a letter to a member of the Elsternwick Club he wrote:

> The days I remember most were as a kid in and around Elsternwick – more than some of my better known days in Test cricket. It was at Elsternwick State School and the Elsternwick cricket ground and the little ground at the back adjoining the big ground that I learned most of my cricket.

Already he had discovered a hero – Bill Ponsford. Ponsford's home was only a quarter of a mile away and Miller would often go past his house in order to catch a glimpse of him. Even when Ponsford married and moved to Glenhuntly, a remoter place, Miller made the trek. Following his brothers' advice, he watched 'Ponny's' style. Though an attractive player, Ponsford was essentially an accumulator whose statistical feats of run-gathering were eclipsed only by Bradman.

In 1934 as Miller entered Melbourne High, the next step on the academic ladder, he met his mentor: Bill Woodfull, a teacher at the school and captain of Australia. Woodfull was known as the 'unbowlable', and A. G. Moyes likened his back-swing to 'a man opening a door an inch or two, then closing it hurriedly so that nothing could enter'. Subsequently he did develop a run-getting appetite but he always remained consistent, patient, watchful: ever the school-master.

These two influences are interesting and significant because of their effect on the young Miller and the contrast they provide to his later career. Determined, watchful, reliable are adjectives that recur in his early cricket career. Then after the war, they are replaced by that single, distinctive, probably over-worked word: cavalier. Perhaps Miller's subsequent approach was in part an unconscious rejection of the processes that were such a prominent feature of Australian batting before the war. While he was being schooled in cricket the Australian run-machines became operational: the Woodfull-Ponsford opening partnerships, Ponsford's remorseless run records and of course Don Bradman. The last two were to exercise a tremendous psychological hold over England, and not merely in cricket. When Italy fell during the war a Tory MP said, 'We've got Ponsford, now we have to get Bradman.'

Melbourne High – its motto was 'Honour Their Work' – was a strict, almost staid, school. It conveyed the flavour of a healthy mind in a healthy body. Its sporting instincts were strong; its library had 700 books from the *World of Tomorrow* to the story of the Tests in England; and its socials were noted, according to *Unicorn*, the school magazine, for 'an obvious scarcity of Romeos and Casanovas, and a predominance of Galahads'. This was somewhat compensated for by the supper.

It was a State-supported institution, there were no tuition fees, and Miller was no scholastic giant. He spent three years here – 1934 to 1936 – two of them in Form 3, failing to open his account in Geometry one year but showing a greater appetite for languages. Of course, there was sport: Australian Rules football, baseball and cricket.

In the absence of Woodfull due to cricket duties, George Stirling often supervised the coaching of the first eleven:

At the beginning of one year I was trying out the new pupils who thought they had a chance of making the first eleven. After watching a few I was greatly impressed by one fair-haired lad who played with a delightfully straight bat. I asked him who coached him and his reply was, 'Oh, I play with my brother in the backyard'.

So Miller became a member of the first team although he was only a third-former.

Miller soon established a reputation as a determined, reliable batsman. His first captain at Melbourne High was Bluey Truscott. Truscott, who was later to reveal a remarkable flair for combat and was killed during the war in almost legendary circumstances, was greatly impressed by him. This is what he said in one of his team talks as captain of the School XI in 1934:

> The way you fellows went on to the ground yesterday made me weep. What's wrong with your mothers? Haven't you got an iron in the house? Haven't you got a bottle of brilliantine? Let's have some spit and polish. Anoint your heads and crease your flaming pants. Jack Hobbs always used to say, 'If you can't be a cricketer, at least look like one'. Do you see me walking round with grease stains on the seat of my strides or with baggy knees, or a dirty neck? So help me, I was ashamed of you.
>
> And when I say smarten up that means in all departments. Don't be scared to have a go. Pin your ears back and get stuck into it. If you can't bowl a man out, bluff him out. Now this business of Keith Miller is the case in point. Miller's only a little squirt, but he stands up to the lot of you and beats the hell out of you. The unbowlable Keith Miller! Yes, he's got a stout defence and the heart of a lion.

Batting was by no means easy. *Unicorn* recorded in July 1935: 'As the matches were all one-day affairs, the innings had often to be closed before some of the batsmen could settle down'.

That year Melbourne High retained the school trophy and Miller, in the match that decided the championship, made 30 in a winning score of 127.

By 1936 Miller was opening the innings. When the school

played the Royal College from Colombo, in a match widely advertised as one of the 'ties that bind the Empire', he, with 28 not out in a school score of 74 for 5, prevented a 'Cingalese' (*Unicorn*'s spelling) victory. He and the other players were rewarded with a dinner with Woodfull and a visit to the popular Regent Theatre.

Yet Miller's cricket future was by no means certain, nor cricket his dominant interest. Years later he was to write: 'When I was a kid scoring a century ... was never my ambition at all, but rather to ride the winner of the Melbourne Cup ...' – which, in popularity and appeal is the Australian equivalent of the Grand National. The Caulfield racecourse was within easy walking distance of his house and he would often go there to watch the horses gallop and hope to catch the eye of the trainers. 'I used to pay two bob a time and go and borrow a horse from the local riding school and belt it round the streets of the Melbourne suburb of Caulfield.'

Two other factors seemed to conspire against his becoming a cricketer. He was now sixteen but still a little over five foot tall and he did not weigh a great deal: ideal physique for a jockey. Also, he had suffered set-backs at the hands of the Melbourne cricket clubs. At the age of thirteen he had applied to the St Kilda Club. It had superb facilities: three grounds, one of which had four grandstands and a capacity of 40,000, crowd-pulling players and five teams. Miller could not find a place even in the fifth team. The St Kilda selection committee suggested he try again in three years' time.

Miller joined Elsternwick, nearer home. He made his debut in a match where play was possible only on the first day. The opposition batted, Miller fielded on the boundary, did not bowl, did not bat and was dropped from the next match because of his 'slowness in the field'. But some good did come out of all this. There was practice at the backyard net of Bill Nichols and advice from E. V. ('Hughie') Carroll, the Victorian player and South Melbourne coach. Carroll recommended Miller to South Melbourne and he went straight into the first team.

South Melbourne was respectable and in many ways just as

illustrious as St Kilda. Jack Blackham, Spofforth's wicket-keeper, had played for it at the turn of the century, Warwick Armstrong had been captain and when Miller joined, Lindsay Hassett, who was just making a reputation, was a member.

Miller began grade cricket – matches played over two Saturday afternoons – quietly. In his first match he scored 11 in an hour and a half. Then came the last match of the season, against Carlton captained by Bill Woodfull. South Melbourne lost half their side for six runs before Miller, using a specially cut-down bat because of his height, came in.

Under the headline 'The Ranks of Tuscany', a Melbourne daily, in somewhat breathless prose, described the scene:

> To this nerve-taxing situation comes a sixteen-year-old high school pupil making his debut with the district eleven. He faces bowlers who are flushed with a success almost too good to be true. Moreover – what trick of fate provides this acid test? – fielding at mid-on (and other places) is the boy's school-master of international reputation and the safest pair of hands that ever saved a boundary. Small wonder if the bowler, twining strong fingers around the leather, smiles in anticipation of yet another cheap wicket. While there is cricket 'life' there is also cricket hope. And the school-master? What, after all, is he here? Only mid-on & Co., and opposing skipper. No chance of 'detention' from him here. He and his bowlers will claim dismissal the very second they get a ball in among the stumps or their eager hands on a catch. On the other hand one may 'whack' his bowlers to any part of the field and even send him scampering to the fence behind the elusive fourer. The prospect is alluring so let's have a try. And thus develops a performance that tempers, with smiles and encouraging praise, the spirit of the unrelenting bowling attack. This cricket Horatius is a foe worthy of anybody's willow. Instead of South Melbourne sustaining sensational defeat in one day the score is advanced to a state that requires the personal attention of the schoolmaster—captain and an experienced lieutenant at the wickets for half the second afternoon before Carlton's victory is assured.
>
> Meanwhile, the youthful Keith Miller caps his gallant forlorn hope of 61 not out by taking a Carlton wicket at a cost of 7 runs. No wonder the ranks of Carlton do not forbear to cheer.

The next day Woodfull presented him with an engraved egg-shaped cup, specially awarded for 'sterling performance'. It was the only cup he ever received, and his one other cricket trophy was a clock for heading the batting averages with Melbourne Colts some years later.

Now fate intervened. Within the space of a year – the ages of sixteen and seventeen – Miller gained more than a foot in height. There is no apparent reason why he should have so suddenly and spectacularly increased his height apart from one possible factor: he had given up smoking. Between the ages of ten and twelve he was a chain smoker. One day he smoked a cigar, was sick, and has never smoked since.

So, with the passion for racing confined to an active interest in starting prices, he began to establish his cricket reputation. In February 1938 he made his debut in the State side. Victoria played Tasmania in one of the traditional matches played to foster the game – Tasmania was not then a member of the Sheffield Shield – and Miller made 181. But it was the last week of December and it was another season before he played again for Victoria. Again, the opponents were Tasmania.

Victoria were in the middle of a sponsored tour of Tasmania followed by Western Australia – then not a member of the Sheffield Shield and trying to provide first-class opposition for its inexperienced players. Miller had a mixed tour. He made 38 and 55 in the first of the two matches against Western Australia. In three other matches his highest score was 17, though he was twice not out in incomplete innings. At the end of the season he had made 125 runs in seven innings for an average of 25.00. But the Victorian selectors were convinced of his potential and next season he was promoted to the full State team.

Miller's first match was against South Australia at Adelaide. Here he met a future friend, played against Don Bradman and learnt a cricketing lesson. The friend to be was Richard Whitington. Years later they were to play together in the Victory Series, and later still Whitington was to act as his journalistic mentor and co-author seven books with him. But on 17 November 1939 Miller had made 4 when he edged

Cotton, the South Australian fast bowler, to slips and Whitington made no mistake.

The cricketing lesson was provided by Clarrie Grimmett in the second innings. Miller had made 7 when he played back and was bowled. Grimmett took the wickets of three other Victorians who were also making their debuts and the next day a newspaper published a photograph of the dismissals under the headline, 'Grimmett's bag of youngsters'. Miller made a mental note: all of them had played back. A month later in the return match at Melbourne he played forward consistently and made 108.

In both matches he had been involved with Bradman. In the first match he ran Bradman out. An Australian observer described the effect:

A telegraphic error was suspected when the incredible tidings came from one Adelaide match that Bradman had been run out. Statisticians had to go back 10 years to find the last time he was a victim of between-wicket misunderstanding in these inter-state matches.

In the return match, after Miller had made his century, he played what he thought was a bump ball into Bradman's hands. Bradman said, 'Oh, well bowled'. The implication was obvious and the umpire gave Miller out. It was his first experience of the way the game was played at the highest level.

Miller played seven other innings, finding the Queensland attack friendly – 41, 47 not out and 37 – the New South Wales one less so – 14, 14, 1 and 24 which was not surprising. Against New South Wales he had encountered possibly the most combative cricketer in the history of the Australian game, Bill O'Reilly, and O'Reilly was to take his wicket twice (Cec Pepper took it on the other occasions). Spin, in fact, had been a major Miller problem: in ten dismissals he had fallen to spinners six times and at the end of the season the statistical rewards were limited. In eleven innings, once not out, he had made 298 runs averaging 29.80.

But in a season dominated by the greats of Australian

cricket (Bradman headed the table with 1,062 runs for an average of 132; O'Reilly with 52 wickets was just ahead of Grimmett with 49) he had done enough to show his potential. *The Cricketer's* Australian correspondent described him as 'a tallish, young stylist who jumps into the ball confidently. In his backfoot cover strokes he seems merely to brush the ball away to get boundaries.' Bradman had made encouraging noises after his innings of 108, while Clem Hill was certain that 'the boy will bat for Australia'. Hill had been particularly impressed by the way Miller stood over the ball and forced it wide of mid-on or mid-off. And his fielding, particularly in the covers, had also elicited praise. But there was no mention of the bowler. Though Victoria had at times used as many as seven bowlers, Miller had bowled just one over.

Miller had given little thought to bowling. Batting was his prime aim. He usually batted no. 3 or 4, his early heroes – Ponsford and Woodfull – were specialist batsmen, and his height, till the age of sixteen, discouraged fast bowling. When he was trying to join St Kilda, Heck Oakley, a Victorian hitter, had admonished him, 'Child, hand the ball to someone who can bowl'. Later, Hughie Carroll, who recommended him to South Melbourne, had advised slow bowling. He had occasionally come on as the fifth or sixth change, but without conspicuous success.

Then in 1940 came the war benefit match between Bradman's XI and Stan McCabe's XI. Miller started the match as a batsman but suddenly both the opening bowlers broke down. One of the players pointed at him and said, 'This fellow might be able to sling 'em down'.

Grimmett, who was captaining the side, took a good look then said, 'You are big and strong. Try to bowl'.

Miller, who confesses, 'I had never bowled properly before', decided to go for sheer speed. He took the wicket of Ken Riddings, then Bradman came in. Bradman was on a pair: he edged Miller but O'Reilly at slip dropped the catch.

Australian cricket could provide no further opportunities to develop what was obviously a natural talent. The consequences of a world war had already caught up with the game. The Shield had been formally suspended for the duration of the war soon after the end of the 1939-40 season and with cricket reduced to Saturday afternoon frolics, Miller now turned to his other great interest – Australian Rules football. That year he joined St Kilda Football Club. He played in the senior eighteen till he left Australia in 1942. He was to play for St Kilda after the war, represent Victoria and, when he moved to Sydney, New South Wales in inter-state football. It was in 1947, when he injured his ankle in the All-Australian match at Hobart, that he finally gave up the game.

In a letter on behalf of the Club, Jules Feldman writes:

> Keith was an outstanding exponent of Australian Rules football and played in most positions of the field earning a special reputation as a full forward and also as a full back. He was noted for his long, accurate kicking and frequently covered distances of seventy yards or more. Strong and fearless, he played the game with great spirit – something which was acknowledged (sometimes ruefully) by his opponents. Had he not given up his football career to concentrate on cricket he would most certainly have won an even greater reputation for his football . . . Victorian league football attracts very large crowds and Keith during his playing years with our club was recognised as one of our most gifted footballers. In any case, he is still very well remembered as a footballer by our older supporters.

But going back to 1940 and cricket, Miller had arrived at the gate marked Promise. The war and his experiences in it were to provide the means for a triumphant entry.

3

Fate in the form of an extraordinary increase in height had determined his sporting career: youthful loyalty was to decide his war effort. Miller and Johnny Hosking, a friend who was very keen to go to sea, applied to the Navy for jobs as stokers. Miller was accepted; Hosking was not. Hurt and angry at the brusque treatment meted out to his friend, Miller walked out of the Naval recruiting office. There the friends parted. Miller applied to the Royal Australian Air Force, Hosking joined the Army and vanishes from our story. But he had played a part in a decision which was to have dramatic effects on Miller's career.

The RAAF did not call on him for some time, and while he waited for the call there was a wide variety of jobs: in the spare parts section of a motor business, as a customs and shipping agent and with the Vacuum Oil Company. There was also Saturday afternoon cricket and Australian Rules football. On 30 January 1942 the RAAF enlisted him as a Trainee Aircrew. There followed training spells in different parts of the country and for a time he was stationed at his favourite Caulfield racecourse. Here an indulgent sergeant allowed him to lay bets for him but when he consistently backed losers the sergeant lost a great deal of his enthusiasm.

On 12 November 1942 Miller was awarded his pilot's Flying Badge and now events moved swiftly. On 15 January 1943 he sailed for America en route to the United Kingdom. This, for a young man of twenty-three, abroad for the first time, was indeed the New World. There was the transition from an Australian summer to a North American winter – the first memory of snow was to remain for a long time – and there was a brunette: Peggy Wagner, a brown-eyed girl with wealthy connections who worked as a secretary at the Massachusetts Institute of Technology. In that New England winter Miller took her to Boston symphony concerts and formed a close attachment.

Two months later he sailed for Britain or, more precisely, Greenock in Scotland. It was a typical wartime crossing of the Atlantic. The *Queen Elizabeth* was packed, occupation of bunk space was limited to eight hours, the atmosphere was hot and humid and nobody apart from air-spotters was allowed on deck.

After all this Britain was a great relief, an unexpected relief. He had read the grim stories and heard the Blitz news but at the first touch of reality the image of a beleaguered island dissolved. He was moved by the warmth and generosity of the welcome. The South Coast hit-and-run raids had begun – fighter-bombers dropping a few bombs, machine-gunning a town and streaking off – and he soon found himself in Bournemouth. He was to spend his entire active service in the South.

Soon after he arrived in Bournemouth, he was invited one weekend to play for the RAAF at Dulwich. That Sunday afternoon a hit-and-run raider bombed a bar that was a particular Miller haunt. Had he not been playing cricket he would certainly have been there. Six or seven of his friends were killed.

Soon afterwards Miller was flying a Beaufighter on a routine exercise. Suddenly the oil pressure went to zero. He was not particularly worried: the instrument had given him trouble before. Half an hour later another instrument malfunctioned and he decided to fly back to base. On landing he reported the aircraft, the mechanic repaired it and that night another pilot took off in it. He had just got airborne when he reported that something was wrong. He was asked to fly back, crashlanded and was killed. Miller's war had begun, a war that was to provide a uniquely concentrated course in living and dying.

Miller was quick to gain promotions. Within two months

he became a Flight Sergeant, and just over a year after arriving he received his commission. Already he had established a reputation for nonchalance, in a profession where nonchalance was almost second nature. Drama seemed to cling to everything he did.

Returning one dark night from a fairly unremarkable operation, he misjudged the landing, the wheels hit and bounced off the runway. So he tried again. This time only one of the motors picked up speed and, with the surge of power on one side, the aircraft veered across the runway and headed for the hangars. He pulled the stick back and cleared them by inches.

By 1944 Miller, having flown every type of combat aircraft from Tigers and Beauforts to Mosquitos, was firmly established as a Mosquito pilot with 169 Squadron (RAF), flying in support operations with bombers that were said to be pounding Germany to defeat. One particular night he was attacking airfields in the Schleswig-Holstein area near the Kiel Canal. The Mosquitos had drop tanks filled with highly inflammable substances and Mills bombs attached to their wings. The procedure was to drop the tanks as the plane flew low over the target, and when the Mills bombs went off they would ignite the tanks. Miller was closely following this procedure over the target – he was down to about 900 feet – when he found himself under a German searchlight. He extricated himself, pressed the bomb release as per schedule but only one of the tanks fell off. A hail of anti-aircraft fire shot up and would have hit the plane had not the weight of the unreleased tank knocked him off course. Miller recognised the closeness of his escape and he felt that he had secured his operational ration of what he had come to believe in as 'Miller's luck'.

But the unexploded tank was still attached to the wings and all the way back he thought about it. The landing was normal and he indicated to the ground crew that the tank was still on board. He was wrong. The tank had been partly released over Germany and fell off just as he was landing. It had broken to bits, the fluid had spread across the runway but the bombs had failed to explode. The examining officer was incredulous, 'It was a miracle it didn't explode . . . I don't understand it'.

Yet the incident that provided Miller with his wartime reputation and was to have a considerable impact on his career was the result of a prank. The war was almost over and the young airman, broke in London, had a few days' leave still in hand. He returned to camp and decided to take his mechanic – a fellow Australian – for a spin. He overrode the navigator's misgivings about flying during leave and took off.

The flight appeared to be nothing out of the ordinary until he decided to indulge in a spot of low flying. Suddenly he felt a surge on one side of the wing and just managed to stop the aircraft from ploughing into the ground. Then the starboard engine caught fire. The aircraft was of laminated wood but fortunately Miller was able to use the fire extinguisher and cut out both the fire and the engine. He now had to land with the help of one engine. His first attempt was too high and he came in a second time. At the edge of the landing field he could see his friends playing cricket. That, he thought, is where he might have been. As he landed he failed to ground his tail and the plane was still at flying speed, so he retracted the wheel and crashed to the ground. Miller managed to walk away from the crash, quipped 'nearly stumps drawn that time, gents' and was playing soccer within an hour. But there was a reaction. He started getting pains in the back, pains that were to disrupt his subsequent career and once caused him to collapse on the cricket field. The war had provided him with an image but it was to extract its price.

Of course the war was not all scrambling away from ruined Mosquitos and stunts in the air. Nor was Miller the only cricketer to suffer. Hutton had an arm shortened and Hedley Verity was killed.

Yet the experiences remain. Arthur Koestler has called fighter pilots the aristocrats of death. It is a phrase that sums up the image: the romance of combat flying, the myth of independence, the anticipatory thrill of a glamorous, total extinction. In a war where the capacity to produce steel was, perhaps, the final arbiter, Miller's deeds stood out as one of the few individual points of identification. You cannot worship steel, you can admire a man. The war provided him with an aura, one that was to justify his failures and enhance his successes, and one that was all the more singular because none of his contemporaries had remotely comparable experiences. Bedser, Compton, Lindwall, Hutton and Bailey all served in the less glamorous elements of the Armed Forces.

The man followed the image. The technical skills of the cricketer did not change but the individual who lived these experiences learnt to recognise his priorities. Cricket was, after all, a game. He also developed his wider interests and formed one of the closest friendships of his life.

Jean Bowler (*née* Slater) was Flight Driver at the Great Massingham Camp in Norfolk. She would drive the men out to their aircraft and then pick them up after their operations. 'And every time I waved them goodbye it was like a little death.' Today she exudes the feeling that she has seen it all and recalls those years with a warm, never-to-be-repeated satisfaction.

She first met Keith at one of the camp dances. He asked her to dance but was clearly incapable. ('He is a terrible dancer, can't put one foot in front of another.') They went out for air and Keith collapsed. Jean helped him to his bed. He returned the next day to say 'ta', and that was the start of their friendship.

This was the world of Dusty – all his service friends called him that; later his cricket deeds were to inspire another, more flamboyant, name. In the interludes that the war invariably provided Jean and Keith would enjoy simple delights. They would steal WAA bicycles and go for rides in the wilds of Norfolk, there would be apple-picking expeditions and long, lazy convivial sessions at the local pubs. Jean can still recall one in particular, the Crown. 'They prepared a marvellous steak – egg on top and plenty of horseradish to go with it. And in those days Dusty did enjoy his beer.'

The pair discovered that they were born under the same sign and that they shared common interests in classical music and poetry. Many years after the war they were among a group of people discussing poetry. Grey's 'Elegy' was mentioned. A rather sporty lady listened with increasing impatience then blurted out, 'Oh, do stop talking about that bloody poem'. Both of them said, almost simultaneously, 'But that's the epitome of English literature'. (Jean tells this story with a certain amount of relish; she feels Keith's wider interests have not received due recognition.)

There would also be moments of remembrance. Keith would send money to his niece who was about nine and write long, loving letters. Years later when she died of cancer, still a young woman, he was visibly shaken at the injustice.

But he was far from a hero in the camp. He was not even the ladies' first choice. According to Jean Bowler, 'The Squadron Commander, Neville Reed, was considered the Greek God. He was the really handsome bloke.' And in camp cricket Miller was plainly uninterested. In fact cricket during the war did not engage him seriously. Many of the friends who drank regularly with him at the Seven Bells in Brighton – one of his favourite wartime pubs – did not even know that he had played first-class cricket before the war.

War cricket was a minor relief. Though a great many matches were played, particularly at Lord's, it was partly showing the flag and partly a recreation for servicemen in between their tours of duty. The various services organised their own teams, though the Empire XI, which did not owe allegiance to the services, was possibly the most active.

By the time Miller arrived in England the Royal Australian Air Force had enough players to form a team, with Keith Carmody, the New South Wales Sheffield Shield player, as their captain. The Australian Services were not organised to play properly and they displayed a wide and interesting variety of apparel: flannels co-existed happily with drill shorts and service boots. By its very nature the cricket had to be improvised.

On 12 June 1943 Miller opened the bowling for United Services against Sussex at Hove; two days later he played for F/O H. P. Chaplain's XI against Group Captain A. J. Holmes's XI, ten days later, at Horsham, he opened the batting for Sussex against the RAF; a month later he came on as the fifth-change bowler playing for the RAAF against the South of England, again at Hove. In this match the South of England looked as though they might have to choose between two England wicket-keepers, but due to the exigencies of war, they finally took the field with a last-minute choice from Gloucester.

Miller's performance followed a certain pattern. He would bat no. 3 or 4, make a quick 50 or so – it was often the dominant innings of the match – then come on as a relief bowler and turn out to be the fastest. The surprise caused by the power and command of his batting could be tempered by reference to his pre-war Sheffield Shield reputation, but nothing could have prepared England for his bowling.

Trevor Bailey met Miller for the first time in a RAAF v. Navy match at Hove. By the time Miller, as fifth-change bowler, came on to bowl, Bailey, with a reasonable score behind him and the wicket-keeper standing up, was looking forward to some cheap runs. The first ball shot past the stumps for four byes before either Bailey or the wicket-keeper could move.

Compton, playing in a charity match at Lord's, was among the runs when the ball was thrown to Miller almost as an afterthought. Compton turned to Stan Sismey, the wicket-keeper, and enquired about Miller.

'Oh, he's not really a bowler. I expect he wants some exercise, but you might find him a bit quick.'

The ball, delivered from a casual run, was, says Compton, 'the fastest ball bowled to me since I played against Ernie McCormick of the 1938 Australian team to England'.

Jack Andrews met Miller at the Parks at Southampton. The circumstances were casual. Andrews, a useful Hampshire opening batsman, was experienced against pace and Miller, without a proper run-up, just sauntered up to bowl the first ball of the innings. John Arlott, who as substitute fielder claims a 'less subjective experience', describes what happened:

> The ball pitched short and Jack moved into back defensive stroke: but not quickly enough or high enough. The ball lifted almost vertically, flicked his lifted left elbow and cleared the long-leg boundary, a short one but still a long carry off the funny bone.

Later, such things could be viewed with the necessary historical dispassion, perhaps amusement. Compton became a great friend, Bailey a powerful adversary, and even Jack Andrews could recall it in the accepted style: 'I opened the batting against Keith Miller.' But such historical dispassion was at least two years away and critics were not prepared to consider him as a serious bowler. Sir Home Gordon, writing in the *Cricketer Annual* of 1943-44, said: 'My belief is that he has not yet attained his zenith as a bat, but that his bowling will not ahead be regarded as more than a useful change'.

Then these incidents seemed very much part of a personality that, despite the confused and chaotic back-drop, had already begun to make an impression. He would arrive just before a match was to start. He was just as likely to bowl from five yards as from fifteen without any loss of pace. At Hove he became the first batsman to hit two consecutive sixes into the adjoining lawn tennis courts, and in the RAAF v. Navy match, where Bailey met him, he arrived with a shirt slung over his shoulders, a pair of worn boots in his hands and no socks. When asked if he suffered from corns he replied, 'What are corns?'

These were the unrehearsed products of a life-style reduced to the barest essential: survival. Miller, as John Arlott was to write later, 'was busy living life in case he ran out of it'.

There was one other thing: he had fallen under the spell of Lord's. Jack O'Shea, the attendant, had secured him a corner of the dressing room that would be for ever his and that rare prize at Lord's: a shower – Miller having taken a deep and instant dislike to the baths of Lord's. The ground was to make a deep impression on him. Years later he wrote:

> It is the worst feeling in the world to fail at Lord's. First there comes the long straight walk back to the pavilion, followed by what seems the even longer walk through the appropriately named Long Room. You open the door and walk on rubber. You can hear no sound ... The day you walk through an applauding Long Room at Lord's it seems as if you have had a hallmark stamped on your career.

He was rarely, if ever, to fail at Lord's.

His first match there came within two months of his arrival in England. In front of a respectable crowd of 8,231 and for the benefit of the Red Cross he made 45 out of 56 in little over an hour against an attack that consisted of Alec Bedser, Bailey and Gubby Allen.

It was at Lord's in 1944 that Miller made his first substantial impression on the public. The season, such as it was, had begun badly. Keith Carmody, the captain and inspirer of the team, was a prisoner of war with the Germans, flying bombs had made their appearance and Miller and Stan Sismey were the only recognised cricketers in the RAAF team that had been organised the previous April by sorting hundreds of letters that had come in response to a circular. Also, he had torn some ligaments. Then on 15 July Miller made his first century at Lord's. In two and three-quarter hours he made exactly 100 runs, hitting nine fours, the hook and the drive being the main weapons.

Three weeks later, playing for 'Australia' against an 'England' team that included Hammond, Washbrook, Simpson, Edrich, Bailey, Evans and Wright, he made 85. It was the highest score of the innings, and it very nearly secured an Australian victory against the clock. Sir Home Gordon, who was one of the first to 'spot' him, was positively exultant and suggested with more zeal than geographical exactitude that 'I can imagine Cardus describing him as the NSW Constantine'.

By the end of the season Miller had acquired a distinct following at Lord's. More significantly, he had begun to develop a rapport with the crowd, always a distinguishing part of his cricket. When the servicemen thronging the Tavern shouted, 'Give us a bouncer', Miller, realising that many had just experienced more deadly things and some would never again see peace, would instantly oblige.

It was in 1945 that he was to extend his following beyond the narrow geographical confines of the South of England and, largely within the space of six matches, secure his international reputation. Yet the prelude was sombre, and a happy chance provided the stage. On 8 May Germany surrendered. The sudden end of the European war caught the cricket administrators by surprise. The idea of a celebratory series was not new, yet the season had already begun and matches had to be hastily rearranged to fit in a series of five Victory Matches between England and the Australian servicemen already in the country. Both teams faced problems. England had to find a selection committee,

Australia had to choose between two teams – the RAAF and the Australian Imperial Forces, which had recently arrived in England after playing a great deal of cricket in the Middle East – and find a captain. It was a battle between the Australian Air Force and the Australian Army.

Hassett, captain of the AIF team, had been a member of the pre-war Australian team and was widely tipped to succeed Bradman should he retire. Yet Keith Carmody, recently released from a prisoner-of-war camp, had moulded the RAAF, and it was their popularity that was partly responsible for the idea of the Victory series. In the end the Army won on both counts. The AIF contributed a good many of the players. Hassett became captain.

It would be tempting to see this as a happy, carefree series where the sheer joy of being released from more important worries obscured the normal demands of competitive cricket. It was certainly a very happy series – both teams shared the same dressing room – but technical skill was never sacrificed. And the cricket in that period always had a hard competitive edge. Between the Second and the Third Victory Matches the RAAF met the South of England at Lord's. Gubby Allen was batting against Roper, the Australian fast bowler. He was forced into a defensive stroke and the ball rolled back towards his stumps. Allen turned and murmured to the wicket-keeper, 'That was close', picked up the ball and tossed it back to Roper. Roper appealed, and the umpire had no option but to give Allen out, handled the ball, one of the rarest forms of dismissal and something always considered less than fair. Then, while the booing of the 11,000 crowd held up play, Miller ran after Allen and unsuccessfully tried to coax him to return.

In general the cricket authorities took the matches seriously. The Australian authorities were so concerned about the class of their representation – Hassett was the only Test player, though five others had played pre-war first-class cricket – that they refused to grant the matches official Test status. And England fielded her strongest possible side, as can be seen from the teams that lined up for the First Victory Match:

England	_Australia_
L. Hutton	Flt Sgt J. A. Workman
Flt Sgt C. Washbrook	Capt R. S. Whitington
Capt J. D. Robertson	W/O A. L. Hassett
Sqn Ldr L. E. G. Ames	Sqn Ldr G. Sismey
W. R. Hammond	P/O K. R. Miller
Sqn Ldr W. J. Edrich	F/O R. L. Stanford
Sqn Ldr R. W. Robins	Sgt C. G. Pepper
Lt-Col J. W. A. Stephenson	Capt A. G. Cheetham
Lt-Col S. C. Griffith	W/O R. G. Williams
Lt D. V. P. Wright	Sgt C. F. Price
A. R. Gover	F/O R. S. Ellis

England played seven established Test players, and barring Stephenson all the non-Test cricketers were soon to play regular Test cricket. During the series England called on twenty players, only five of whom never played Test cricket; Compton was the only established player who did not play. Of the fourteen Australians who played, only Hassett and Miller had either a Test past or a Test future.

Even as the Australians took the field for the First Victory Match they were deeply pessimistic about their chances. Richard Whitington, who opened the innings in all five Victory Matches, wrote: 'In their hearts was a deep and haunting misgiving that they might all make fools of themselves'. But, largely owing to Miller, that was to be the last moment of Australian pessimism.

In the First Victory Match at Lord's, after England had made 267 on a 'green' pitch, Miller's 105 in 210 minutes (he hit only six fours and his one and only lofted shot produced a simple catch to Ames) was the core of the Australian reply. His allies were Hassett and Stan Sismey. These efforts were magnified by Stanford and Pepper who put on 88 for the ninth wicket, resulting in a substantial lead. Then Cec Pepper, using his height to get considerable purchase for his finger spin, converted the lead into a dramatic six-wicket victory with Pepper himself hitting the winning run off the fourth ball of the last over just before seven o'clock.

Now the great transformation in Miller's career that was to

lift it to another unsuspected plane was about to take place.
Miller the opening bowler emerged.

It happened in the second innings of the Third Victory
Match at Lord's. Australia were sixty behind and would be
required to bat last; England were playing three schoolboys in
the team – Dewes, White and Carr. In the first innings Miller,
still no. 5 in the bowling, had taken the wickets of Dewes and
Carr. There was also the unrelenting campaign of Bob Crisp –
the South African fast bowler turned writer. He had
successfully persuaded Miller to settle on a fifteen-yard run
and he was determined to get him to open the bowling. So as
Dewes came out to bat with Hutton, Hassett gave the new
ball to Miller.

This remains one of the significant moments of his career.
The pre-war testimonial match apart, he had never opened
the bowling in a full-scale representative match. Before this
Victory Match he had bowled 44 overs and taken three for 81.
At Bramall Lane, in the Second Victory Match, which
England won, his pace had impressed the players and enraged
the spectators. Washbrook had been hit on the temple,
Hutton on the forearm, and the Yorkshire crowd had shouted,
'Go off, Larwood.' Yet he had not been seriously considered
as a fast bowler and even at Lord's, as we have seen, it was
expediency that guided Hassett.

But whatever the motives, it paid dividends. Miller
soon bowled Dewes with an out-swinger. For Dewes it
was the start of a less than happy association. He was to
become a regular Miller victim. As he told me, 'Miller was
just too quick'. Miller took two more wickets, that of Edrich,
breaking a threatening stand between him and Hutton, and
later that of Pollard. The denizens of the Long Room echoed,
in more suitable language, the opinion of the Bramall Lane:
fastest since Larwood. In 16 overs he took three for 42,
Cristofani took five for 49, and England were all out for 164,
leaving Australia to get 225 in 300 minutes. Miller made 71 not
out – the highest Australian score of the match – in just under
two hours and Australia won by four wickets.

Just before the fourth match, again at Lord's, Albert

Cheetham, who had opened the bowling with Graham Williams, returned to Australia and Miller was confirmed as the regular opening bowler. But there was a problem. At Lord's, while fielding to his own bowling, he had strained a back muscle. From now on his bowling was always to be associated with his back. Over the years it was to cause him considerable pain and earn him snide references: whenever he was reluctant to bowl (and he often was) it was suggested that the real cause was not any physical problems but the Miller temperament.

It is possible that this was not as welcome a moment in Miller's career as is generally supposed. Increasingly his bowling affected his batting – in 1948, as we shall see, most crucially – and he never did recapture his 1945 form. But the argument cannot be resolved. He might have been a more consistent batsman had he never been a bowler, but then some of the most dramatic moments in Test cricket would have been lost.

In the fourth match the Australians were playing to a plan: to place England in a position where Hammond would have to take risks in order to win. In a three-day match the Australians made 388 in a day and a half, with Miller again making the most significant contribution. Using three bats and after overcoming the sharp in-swing of Pope, he made his second century in the series, appropriately in front of the newly elected prime minister, Clement Attlee. His 118 took just under three hours, and with Stan Sismey he put on 121 in two hours. It provided Australia with a valuable advantage. England would have to score heavily and quickly to win. England made 469 but not quickly enough. The plan succeeded and the match was drawn. Australia went into the last match at Old Trafford still leading 2-1.

This match was to see, probably, the most heroic Miller innings of the series. The ground, extensively damaged during the war, had been repaired by German prisoners of war at a cost of three-farthings an hour and the wicket had rolled out a green top. *Wisden* called it a 'natural wicket which encouraged the bowlers and, at times, gave them much assistance'. Hassett won the toss, batted and Australia had lost four wickets for 66 when Miller came in. For the next 135 minutes, while England, using only three bowlers – Pope, Pollard and Phillipson – removed the other six Australian batsmen, Miller made 77 not out while his other colleagues were adding 107 runs to the total. Only two other batsmen made double figures, both of them under 30.

Then, when England batted, Miller with sheer speed tried to right the advantage. He soon removed Fishlock but Hutton and Hammond held firm. The one solidly defensive, the other boldly venturesome saw England first to safety and then to a position from which victory was possible. England led by 70 in the first innings. But at last Miller failed: he made 4. Australia could leave England only 141 to win, and just before the Manchester rain clouds pressed home, England won by six wickets to square the series 2-2.

So at the end of his first series Miller headed the batting with an average of 63.29, his aggregate of 443 was the highest on either side, and his ten wickets were at a very respectable cost of 27 runs each. Outside the Victory Matches his batting displayed its richness in a variety of conditions. Amidst rainstorms and on a muddy Old Trafford pitch he made 52 out of 109 for the RAAF against Lancashire, the only half-century in the match. Against Voce – who took eleven wickets – and on a rain-affected Nottingham wicket he made 81 not out (with two sixes), the highest score of the match between Nottinghamshire and the Australian Services. And on a Sheffield green-top where Bowes took four for 48 he made 111, thrice hitting Booth, the Yorkshire spinner, into the pavilion. None of his colleagues in the Australian Services side passed 30; only Hutton with 111 replied for Yorkshire. Yet Miller's most memorable feat was still to come.

Towards the end of the season England played the Dominions at Lord's. There was cricket diplomacy before the match. Hassett fell ill and a captain had to be found. Constantine, the senior international cricketer, was the natural choice. But this was a Dominion team with Australians, South Africans and New Zealanders in the side, and a black West Indian as captain appeared revolutionary. Sir Pelham Warner went to the dressing room just before the match. He spoke of Constantine's seniority, the position of the cricket world, the importance of the match; he sensed a slight hesitation, then a senior member of the team agreed. Immediately everybody fell in line and Constantine got a great reception from the Lord's crowd.

The match itself provided a fitting climax to the season. 1,241 runs were scored in three days: there was a century by Donnelly, two by Hammond, but Miller played probably the greatest single innings of this period. It started on the evening of the second day, Miller finishing with 61 not out, having hit a six to the top tier of the pavilion. Then, on the morning of the third day, came cricket that moved even Sir Pelham Warner to awe. 'In an experience of first-class cricket of nearly sixty years I have never seen such hitting.'

The bare statistics are inspiring. In ninety minutes he scored 124 runs and, at one stage, in three-quarters of an hour he and Constantine put on 117 runs. On a ground that measures 188 yards by 144 yards he hit six more sixes. One of them carried to Block Q on the right of the pavilion and another landed on the small roof of the broadcasting box above the England players' dressing room. A. E. R. Gilligan was in the box:

> The hit came up over mid-on, rising all the time as it came. On hitting the pavilion it fell into a hole that had been made in the roof of the commentary box by shrapnel and the ball had to be poked out by a stick.

This hit very nearly equalled Albert Trott's record of hitting M. A. Noble, the Australian bowler, over the pavilion, Miller falling short by two feet. Later, experts were to reckon that had the match been played on the more traditional pitch – it was played on an adjoining one with a slightly longer carry – then Miller might have equalled the record. But for Miller 'nearly equal' sounds more appropriate.

Yet this was no indiscriminate hitting. The pedigree of his stroke play was unquestioned – in the opinion of many it

rivalled Hammond – and his command of the bowling quite
exceptional. The principal English sufferers were Wright
and Hollies, and Miller's 185 was made out of a score of 336 in
which only four of his colleagues reached double figures. It
also formed the basis of a narrow Dominion victory.

The innings confirmed all the earlier good notices. In
English eyes he was established as the 'discovery' of the war
years. R. C. Robertson-Glasgow wrote:

> From the moment he takes guard he plays each ball just that much
> below its supposed merits that scratches a bowler's pride . . . It is
> dignity with the brakes off.

C. B. Fry said over the BBC in a broadcast specially directed
to Australian audiences:

> In our eyes Miller is Australia's star turn. We know we have been
> watching a batsman already great who is likely, later on, to
> challenge the feats of Australia's champions of the past. Apart
> from his technical excellence, Keith Miller has something of the
> dash and generous abandon that were part of Victor Trumper's
> charms.

English critics were particularly impressed by his style: it
was so peculiarly English. It was based on forward play,
crowned with that most supreme of cricket strokes, the drive.
His repertoire was extensive. He had a thrilling cut,
embellished at times with, for such a huge frame, a very
delicate late cut. He played shots on both sides of the wicket
but it was the drive, particularly the cover-drive played from
an authoritative, upright stance, that was to become his
signature tune. Yet his tendency to lunge forward did get him
into trouble. Often he lunged so far forward that he
overbalanced and fell. In the Oval Test of 1948 he went
forward to Hollies and Evans stumped him. A photograph
(plate 8) catches the moment immediately after the event.
Miller appears to be at the start of a press-up. Over the years
Miller's batting was to change in only one respect: he
discarded the hook. And the man who was intimately

associated with bumpers was often uncomfortable against them. 'Miller cut rather an inept figure himself against the bouncer. He didn't like them,' as Fingleton wrote years later. But that came much later.

Now Miller was established as the great contemporary hero – that is not too strong a word. It was a happy fusion of technical eloquence and distinctive physical attributes, one in particular: his hair. All cricketers exhibit mannerisms but Miller's hair, and what he managed to do with it, became so intimately associated with his cricket that even in retrospect it is difficult to separate it from his play. It was dark and, for the period, long. It seemed to be everywhere: falling over his face as he batted, tossing in the air as he ran up to bowl. Every now and again he would sweep it back with an elaborate gesture. This, in the final analysis, set his cricket following apart from that of his contemporaries. For young boys he was something out of *Boy's Own* paper, the one cricketer likely to sustain fantasy. The weight of the applause probably never matched Bradman's but the shrillness revealed the anticipatory thrill. For young girls there was his undoubted sexual appeal: they would send him letters, offer him chewing gum (he was an addict by now) and follow his every move. At that time, no doubt, some of his gestures, like tugging at his sleeve as he went out to bat or scanning the sky for aeroplanes as he fielded, were signs of nervousness – he was still unused to crowd adulation – but later they were to become deliberate instruments of crowd control. And like all good and genuine heroes he encountered disapproval: hair clips through the post.

The Golden Boy had emerged, and Nugget was to be his nickname for the rest of his career.

*   *   *

It is early autumn 1945. The Australian Services face another six months of cricket. Next stop India. The team are due to leave London by train for Liverpool where a ship awaits them. Two minutes remain for the train to leave, the luggage has been carefully packed away, all the players have taken their seats but there is no Nugget. Then, with his colleagues almost past despair, he arrives carrying a weekend bag – and no bat. He is to go through the whole tour without a bat of his own.

Two months later, an Indian winter day in Calcutta. Miller comes to the crease with Whitington's spare autograph bat. He has taken to a great deal of cross-bat hitting and Whitington is worried. 'I'll be very careful', promises Miller and then, as a helpless Whitington watches from the other end, he proceeds to hit the next four balls of the first over from Mankad into the pond beyond the stand.

This was to be his most satisfying innings of the tour – 82 – and apart from 106 in three hours against the West Zone at Bombay, the cricketer did little. The placid wickets did not aid his bowling, he was unable to bowl in one of the representative matches, and his batting never matched his English form. But if the statistical joys were limited – 470 runs for an average of 36.15, thirteen wickets at a cost of 13 runs each – there were compensations.

India for the Australians was another world. There was cricket legend and there was fantasy. Duleep, with whom Miller became very friendly, met the ship as it arrived at Bombay, and in their first match at Lahore there were vultures in the sky and Sikh military bands playing Scottish medleys and nostalgic lyrics like 'Lili Marlene'.

Indian maharajas still dominated the cricket scene. They had nurtured Indian cricket and though their playing skills were limited their enthusiasm could not be faulted. The Australians encountered the Patialas, one of the most powerful of Indian princely families. Once a young bowler had appealed against the old maharaja for lbw. He was taken to one side by his skipper and reprimanded. 'His Highness decides when he wants to get out. If you wish to be seated beside one of the prettier guests at dinner this evening, I suggest you bear this in mind.' The maharaja eventually gave his wicket away after making 40; the bowler was suitably rewarded. The young Maharaja of Patiala was still active in cricket and Miller played against him. The maharaja fielded some fifteen yards from the bat and what his six-foot-seven frame could not collect his younger brother Rai Singh, fielding behind him, took.

India then was caught up in the final struggle between the Raj, still persevering with its traditions, if somewhat tarnished, and the masters who were to supplant it. In Calcutta on the first day of the match between the Australians and the East Zone there was a riot: twenty-three wickets fell, eight men were killed.

The next day while Denis Compton, on Army service in India and playing for the East Zone, was on 88, anti-British demonstrators marched on to the ground and their leader said to Compton: 'You very good player. You play good innings for us. But you must go'.

Hassett intervened. He asked the leader, 'Do you have a cigarette?'

There followed a frantic search; Pankaj Gupta, Secretary of the Indian Board of Control, did some lobbying, Compton stayed and play resumed. But the demonstration leader's word became something of a joke and formed part of the essential by-play between Miller and Compton whenever they played against one another.

From India the Australians flew to Colombo where Miller, revelling in the atmosphere and the ground conditions, hit 132 and then made arrangements to leave on a Liberator for Freemantle. He arrived at the airport with six huge elephant-hide bags. Flights were difficult to get and he had jokingly mentioned the possibility of smuggling some of his 'cobber' friends on board. Seeing the bags, his colleagues thought that perhaps he was serious after all. The bags were opened: five of them were empty. The mystery was solved only when it was realised that Christmas was a few days away and Miller, who had not been home for three years, wanted to catch up with some shopping at Freemantle.

But Freemantle did not mean rest. The Services side had returned with a huge reputation: their performance in England had been surprising and they were expected to revolutionise the game in Australia. But, tired after their arduous travels and pitted against cricketers eager to prove themselves, their tour was to prove disastrous. New South Wales and Victoria beat them by an innings and Queensland also came close to beating them. Miller alone maintained his reputation. With the bat he averaged 57 in six matches and there was one moment of brilliance. At Sydney against O'Reilly and Lindwall he made 105 while his colleagues made 94, hitting 32 out of a last-wicket stand of 35 and moving Alan Kippax to ecstasy. 'Australia has found another champion,' he said.

His bowling was much less productive, partly because of poor fielding support. His English bowling reputation had considerably surprised Australians, and as the Services side came to Sydney there was intense speculation. Barnes had been scoring prodigiously in the club games, the Sydney pitch was genuinely fast and Miller was bet £5 that Barnes would score a century against him. Barnes cut Miller's fifth ball straight to Hassett. Hassett dropped it. Miller lost the bet.

The match has a more historic significance. Lindwall revealed his potential as a great fast bowler and that weekend Miller met Lindwall. They were to become inseparable friends. For the next ten years – till Miller's retirement – they were to borrow each other's clothes, share rooms on their trips together, pocket one another's change and socialise together: wherever Miller went, Lindwall was bound to follow. Soon they were to form one of the most memorable opening attacks in the history of the game.

Miller was an automatic choice for the tour to New Zealand that followed, but Hassett was the only other member of the Services side that made the team. The cricket on this tour was never serious, the consequences generally negligible. The team found their blazers bore the cryptic label, 'ABC', instead of the more traditional coat of arms of the Australian Cricket Board. As the Australians, to quote Ian Johnson, 'partied their way across New Zealand', it was nicknamed the 'Australian Broadcasting Commission' and even the 'Australian Bottle Company'. Most of the games were played in a festive spirit and the Australians won all their five matches, Miller making 139 in the first match.

The only Test, at Basin Reserve, Wellington, was affected

by rain. Miller did not bowl in the first innings when O'Reilly and Toshack were enough to bowl out New Zealand for 42. Miller made 30 in an Australian score of 199 for 8 declared and in the second innings opened the bowling with Ray Lindwall. He had bowled six overs for six runs and had taken two wickets to reduce New Zealand to 12 for 3 when his back 'went'. But O'Reilly and Toshack once again got among the wickets and Australia won easily.

The real significance of the tour lay in the pointers for the future. It marked the end of Bill O'Reilly's Test career – his knee finally gave way – the start of the Miller-Lindwall combination and the beginning of Australia's post-war cricket supremacy.

But at that stage thoughts of the hard campaign ahead were far away. This was a tour and a season to be enjoyed. A certain spontaneous joy seemed to touch the cricket. The constraints imposed by war were being lifted, simple delights were reappearing without any layered, inhibiting gloss. Never again was cricket to exhibit that zest nor, perhaps, Miller play with the same abandon. Test cricket was to impose conditions, its penalties as well as its pleasures.

5

Miller had returned to an Australia that had experienced war psychosis but not the physical war itself. Damage to Darwin apart, there were no bomb sites, no ruined cities, no scars on the landscape caused by enemy action. This was an advantage – crowds eager for vicarious thrills immediately adopted him – yet it caused problems. The Vacuum Oil Company was still there with a job for him but they wanted him to go to one of their suburban installations at Yarraville. The cushy jobs in and around Melbourne had been filled during the years he had been away by men whose contribution to the war was long-distance sympathy rather than actual physical effort. Miller resented this and held out for some time but, finally, the logic of his financial position could not be escaped.

He lasted in Yarraville for two months. Peggy Wagner and Boston began to appear increasingly attractive. A ship was leaving for San Francisco and he applied for leave to get married. The response was predictable. Miller had been away for a long time, was it not time he settled down? Did some work? Miller resigned. He reckons it was the best thing he ever did and in September 1946 he sailed for America.

His troubles were by no means over. Immigration at San Francisco was difficult. Why did he want to enter America? To get married. What proof did he have that he wanted to return to Australia? Then he remembered a letter from a Victorian Government official stating that he would be wanted to play against the 1946-47 MCC tourists. Immigration was satisfied and Miller got married.

The Millers arrived back in Australia in October 1946, just a few days before Hammond's team was to play Victoria. The

cricket matched his personal mood – still enjoying his
honeymoon – and it confirmed the purpose of the tour: a
goodwill mission to restore international cricket, to reinforce
old imperial and historical ties.

The English cricket authorities had been most reluctant to
send a team. Recovery from the effects of the war was slow
and there were still no conceivable replacements for several
key pre-war players. Verity and Farnes of the immensely
strong and well-balanced 1938 team had died during the war;
Bowes was thirty-seven, not an age which could sustain long
spells of fast bowling – he had also suffered three years as a
prisoner of war – and Hammond was in his forties. But the
swift and complete collapse of the Japanese, the personal
appeal of the Australian deputy prime minister, Dr Evatt, and
the urgings of the Australian Board of Control overruled these
misgivings. Hammond promised his men 'the happiest six
months of their lives', and, transplanted from a rationed, wet
England to a warm Australian summer, the players reacted
understandably. Cliff Cary, the Australian broadcaster,
wrote, 'In between meals they were forever eating fruit, cakes
and chocolates.' Voce and Pollard put on nearly two stone in
weight and another player confessed that he was consuming
more in one day than his full weekly ration in London.

Then came the First Test at Brisbane. Australia won the toss
and had lost two wickets for 74 when probably the most far-
reaching event of the early years of post-war cricket occurred.
Bradman on 23 cut a ball from Voce, Ikin at second slip claimed
a catch, Bradman stayed and the umpire agreed with him. At
the end of the over Hammond, who had watched impassively
from first slip, said to Bradman, 'What a bloody way to start a
series'. The honeymoon was over. The only other occasions
when the two captains exchanged words were when they
tossed.

Later during the series there were to be at least one further
debatable decision about Bradman, light appeals by Barnes
that smacked of gamesmanship and controversy regarding the
use of the bumper. At the end of it the editor of *Wisden* wrote,
'This series has not re-captured the spirit of cricket'.

Though the bowling of Miller and Lindwall aggravated matters – aggravated be it noted, not caused – Miller's personal relations were unaffected. He was just beginning to develop his friendship with Compton and the Bradman-Hammond feud belonged to the generation that had preceded him. He identified with neither, though he held definite views. He was convinced that Bradman was out and his memories of Hammond were warm and friendly. In the Fourth Victory Match of 1945 Stan Sismey had injured himself. Jimmy Workman kept wicket and, confronted with a volatile Miller, gave away 27 byes. That evening Hammond told the Australians: 'There is only one thing preventing you from using Carmody [the twelfth man and a useful keeper], that is my permission and you have it'.

Bradman went on to make 187, convinced himself he had a future in cricket, and was finally out with Australia 322 for 3. Miller, required to consolidate the position, made 79 and put on 106 with Hassett. While Hassett thrived on dropped chances, Miller did not give any and drove beautifully to score his fifty in eighty minutes. And he hit a six over long-on and on to the roof of the members' stand which, observers said, was the largest hit seen at Brisbane's Woolloongabba ground.

The Australians finished with 645. Then came rain to produce – there being no covers – that rare and most vicious of wickets, a Brisbane 'sticky'. For England it could not have come at a worse moment, yet the Australian winter had been unusually dry and the spring had produced a heat-wave, so much so that the Brisbane ground authorities had decided to get a bore sunk at the ground to draw up the hundreds of thousands of gallons necessary to get the wicket and outfield ready for Test cricket.

Miller, switching to off-breaks, was able to make the ball rear and bounce to alarming heights and with Ernie Toshack completed a massive Australian victory by an innings and 332 runs.

In the first innings he took seven for 60; Toshack three for 17; in the second he took two for 17, Toshack six for 82. But Miller's victims were batsmen higher up the order. He took the wickets of Hutton (twice), Washbrook (twice), Compton, Edrich, Ikin and Gibb – Bedser was his only tail-ender.

This search for quality was always to be a major factor in his bowling career. Generally, successful fast bowlers make the initial break-through, remove nos. 1, 2 or 3, then come back and take care of the tail. Miller consistently sought out batsmen who matched his skill.

This Test Match produced one other significant factor. It marked the proper beginning of the Lindwall-Miller partnership, their use of the bumper and their great post-war duels with Hutton. Before the rain and for a time after it, on a wicket which still had the weekend growth of grass – Bradman did not have the wicket shaved or rolled before the day's play – the pair used the short ball tellingly.

Lindwall was probably quicker; Miller used the short ball more frequently. One observer opined that if a line had been drawn half-way down the wicket most of Miller's deliveries would have landed on his own side of that line. Yet the effect was uniform and extremely unsettling for the batsman. One ball would be of regulation length, another would shoot through to the keeper, a third would skid or pop and Hutton was left performing gymnastics of a high, if unbatsmanlike, order.

In the first innings of this First Test, Hutton was bowled by Miller for 7, Washbrook had his cap knocked off by a bouncer and Edrich made 16 in 105 minutes, suffering an estimated forty body blows. Norman Preston – now editor of *Wisden* – who was covering the tour as the Reuters Exchange Telegraph correspondent, cabled: 'This was indeed bodyline if not the same as caused such a storm on Jardine's tour. It showed that the Australian bowlers can exploit the short bumping ball to intimidate batsmen.'

The bumper can often appear the most deplorable of cricket weapons. The apocryphal story of Ernest Jones bowling a bouncer through W. G. Grace's beard apart (there have been learned dissertations about the incident), its use has always been attended with controversy. Miller was aware of the tactical advantage – 'a lot of bad hookers will try to hook a bouncer and get out' – and he always used it as a test of batting skill, not physical courage. Yet the divide is exceedingly thin and Miller, as was to be the case at Trent Bridge in 1948, was not always able to contain the moral indignation the bumper provoked, though he was often amused by it. In the First Test of the 1950-51 West Indian series (when perhaps Miller and Lindwall over-bowled the bouncer) he bowled three bouncers in one over and was warned. He finished the over with slow off-breaks and, turning to the umpire, said, 'Any objections to that?'

Bodyline was a charge that was always being hurled at Lindwall and Miller, but in this first post-war series history and circumstances conspired to make the controversy all the more acrimonious. Goodwill we have talked about; there was Hutton's war injury which had shortened his left arm, Hammond's inability to retaliate – Voce was too old, Edrich not quick enough – and there was the suggestion of an avenging 'plot'. Australia, victim of the 1932-33 bodyline theory, had now turned aggressor. Hutton, who looked capable of challenging Bradman's pre-war deeds, was to be curbed with bouncers – so ran the theory.

Hutton weighed heavily on Australian minds. That winter Tommy Trinder was entertaining Australian audiences. As English disasters succeeded one another he retorted, 'Bradman? Records? What about the Oval 1938?' It always produced a respectful acknowledgement. Then Hutton had made 364 in an English total of 903 for 7 declared. Bradman in trying to stop Hutton from passing his own record 344 had injured his ankle, did not bat and England had won by an innings and 579 runs. One factor stood out. Hutton had made his runs against medium to slow bowling and the pre-war Australians were convinced that he was vulnerable to pace, particularly the bouncer. Miller confirmed this impression during the Victory Series and Lindwall provided further evidence during MCC's match against New South Wales. Though Hutton emerged with credit – 151 in one innings and 97 in the other – his discomfort against the short ball was evident.

Yet Miller and Lindwall never employed classical bodyline methods: short-pitched bowling to a packed leg-side field. Nor is there any support for the idea that Bradman followed Jardine's example and actively instructed Lindwall and Miller – though he did nothing to stop them. At Old Trafford in 1948, during a particularly vicious Miller spell, Bradman told the victim, Edrich, 'These chaps do get out of control'.

Fingleton – one of the few Australian voices that were raised against the bouncer – remains convinced that Miller and Lindwall bowled as many as Larwood and Voce. Fingleton should know: he opened Australia's innings on four occasions during the bodyline series. Even if the dénouement did not match the violence of 1932-33, the effect on Hutton was considerable.

In his first six innings of the 1946-47 series Hutton made 7, 0, 39, 37, 2 and 40. He was out to Miller thrice, to Lindwall once. Then in the Fourth Test at Adelaide he made 94. But, brought up on Herbert Sutcliffe's 'duck and keep out of trouble' technique of meeting bouncers, there remained the question of honour. On the morning of England's second innings, as Bill Bowes walked with Hutton to the Adelaide ground, he said, 'Tha knows what they're saying, Len? That tha's afeard on 'em.' Hutton paused; on the field he hooked Lindwall and Miller for the first time and went on to make 76; in the next Test he made 122. But the hook remained a rare luxury with Hutton and he never mastered the pair. Certainly he had his share of the glory as in the 1950-51 season, his personal best, but not once did he threaten to emulate the Oval 1938. And through a grim English decade his image remained constant. He was the first and often last line of defence against bowlers who had to be contained if England were to survive.

Only once did Hutton escape. In the Second Test at Sydney in December 1946, opening the English second innings, he made 37 in twenty-four minutes. Then his bat slipped from his hand and he was out: hit-wicket to Miller. In the pavilion older members talked of Victor Trumper – there can be no higher praise – and during the lunch interval Jim Kilburn of the *Yorkshire Post* offered his commiserations. 'It's a pity,' said

Hutton, 'we might have been something today.'

In all those years not once did Miller provoke a smile or even a reaction from Hutton. 'I wanted to put some expression into that face,' wrote Miller later. But the nature of the contest would permit no frivolities and Miller confesses, 'I must say that when I bowled at Len I felt a sense of personal grudge I have never known against any other batsman'.

This was perhaps inevitable. His duels with Hutton were an expression of their contrasting personalities. Hutton's personality, like his technical vocabulary, is spare. There is no redolent imagery, no suggestion of the romantic or the extravagant. When I talked to Hutton about Miller he said, 'I suppose you are looking for anecdotes. Yes, that is what makes books sell. The trouble is, there are too many anecdotes.'

The duels were to create their own legacies. Miller and Lindwall spearheaded the Australian attack through seven victorious series – Australia did not lose one till August 1953. It left in Hutton a belief in fast bowling that he never lost, and was to use effectively in Australia in 1954–55. Then the cycle was complete.

At the end of Miller and Lindwall's first series as a pair, their figures read:

	Overs	Maidens	Runs	Wickets	Average
Miller	122.3	15	334	16	20.87
Lindwall	122.1	20	367	18	20.38

Eleven of Miller's sixteen wickets were from among the major English batsmen: Hutton (thrice), Washbrook and Ikin (twice), Edrich, Compton, Evans and Hardstaff. Twelve of Lindwall's eighteen were from the top drawer: Edrich, Compton, Washbrook and Yardley (twice), Hutton, Hammond, Ikin and Evans.

Miller's batting was also remarkably consistent: apart from 79 in the First Test, he made 40, 33, 34, 141 not out, 23 and 34 not out. With Bradman, Barnes and Morris making copious runs, in only two innings was he called on to do much – the first innings of the Fourth Test and the second innings of the Fifth Test.

In the Fourth Test, the Second having been won by Australia and the Third drawn, England had made 460 and Australia without Barnes had lost Bradman, Hassett and, soon after Miller came into bat, Morris. At 222 for 4 Australia were in some trouble. Miller responded by making 141 not out. His innings contained some of the hardest hitting seen in the series – particularly through the covers – and only Yardley with 'leg-theory' was able to subdue him. There was one moment of pure brilliance: a six off the first ball of the fourth day. The ball landed at the foot of the Vice-regal box, and it caught most of the spectators unaware; they had not yet realised that play had begun. With this innings Miller saw Australia to a lead of 27 and safety. As they were already 2-0 up, a draw in the Fourth Test made an Australian rubber a certainty.

His next decisive batting intervention came on the fifth day of the final Test at Sydney. Australia, left to score 214, were struggling against Bedser and Wright, and when Miller came in to bat at 149 for 3, victory was not yet certain. He survived anxious moments against Bedser then swiftly launched a counter-attack. Again the drive was the main weapon, again it succeeded. He shared his enjoyment of the game: he completed one run with a half somersault and, while McCool made the winning hit, he stole a stump as a souvenir for Denis Compton.

Miller finished the 1946-47 series with his status as the world's leading all-rounder confirmed: he was second in both the batting and bowling averages. His 384 runs for an average of 76.80 was some way behind Bradman's 680 runs for an average of 97.14, but better than Barnes, Morris and Hassett; only a decimal point kept him behind Lindwall in the bowling averages.

His Sheffield Shield season was, if anything, even more successful. His batting average of 133.40 was third in the country after Loxton and Hassett; his aggregate of 667 in six innings was easily the highest. There was his innings of 188 at

Adelaide, which was described as one of the finest innings seen at Adelaide; his 153 against New South Wales at Melbourne when he hit Toshack for three sixes, moving his old hero Bill Ponsford to remark that those were the most powerful strokes he had seen; and his 206 not out against the same opponents at Sydney – this time his driving fetched three sixes and fifteen fours. In only one innings did he fail to reach double figures. As a bowler he was used in short, sharp spells by Hassett and in 65.4 overs he took ten wickets at an average cost of 23.

But outside cricket there were problems. He was without a job and he began to consider seriously a move to England. League cricket provided a traditional home for overseas players and Rawtenstall of the Lancashire League had offered such a tempting contract – £1,000 for three seasons – that Miller had signed. It was an amazing situation: Australia's greatest all-rounder unable to get a job in his native country and forced to emigrate to the enemy's stronghold. This damaging Australian paradox had dominated much of the off-field cricket gossip during the 1946–47 season. The President of the Victorian Cricket Association, Dr R. L. Morton, publicly appealed for a job for Miller, and on the eve of the Second Test in Sydney, Mr W. J. Stack, a Sydney businessman, told journalists that he had one of several jobs for Keith Miller in his motor-car agency firm. So while Rawtenstall worried about their contract, Miller himself played it cagily. He told Dr Morton that if something could be arranged he would be anxious to stay in Australia but when an English newspaper asked him what he intended to do he replied: 'I just cannot say one way or the other. You will appreciate my position.'

Miller's reaction was understandable. The Australian public had always distrusted transfers to League cricket which in the past had removed a fair number from the mainstream of their own game. In the winter of 1946–47 the danger seemed particularly acute. McCool, who held a good job, was said to have received lucrative League offers, Lindwall was out of work and Arthur Morris had confessed how he had had to take unpaid leave from his Sydney

Corporation job in order to play Test cricket (and these long
absences had damaged his career prospects). With Test
cricketers averaging £40 for Tests in which a day's takings, as
in Melbourne in the Third Test of that season, could amount to
£34,000, there were growing fears that many more Australian
Test players might follow Miller's example. Miller himself
had begun to rethink. There were persistent rumours that the
Australian Board of Control had threatened to drop him if he
went to Rawtenstall; a newspaper cartoon showed a man in a
raincoat holding a pistol to Miller's head as he was about to set
foot on a ship bound for England; his wife did not fancy the
move and there were more job offers. Finally Miller decided
to accept one as a salesman for cordials and mineral waters and
remain in Australia.

The Rawstensall Secretary, Mr G. Whittaker was not
amused. He threatened to 'call a public meeting and give the
whole story of the negotiations' and finally persuaded the
Lancashire League to ban Miller. The row continued till his
visit to England in 1948 when Rawstenstall settled the alleged
breach of contract, out of court, for £50.

But the job meant a move to Sydney and that brought its
own complications. South Melbourne, who had last won the
first-grade cricket pennant in the days of Miller's old school-
master, Woodfull, were well in the running for the honours.
By the time Miller left he had played in nearly three-quarters
of the club's programme and only two matches were left
before the final rounds. South Melbourne had given him his
first chance in cricket, had helped him on his way to the top.
The move was seen as a great betrayal. Even years later,
whenever, he returned, he could feel a distinct 'atmosphere'.

Miller's move was also part of a wider quarrel: the
intense and historic rivalry between New South Wales and
Victoria. In 1878 the ship carrying the Australian team to
England encountered a terrific storm. 'Suppose we are
wrecked, what would you do,' Spofforth, probably the
greatest Australian bowler of the classical age, enquired of
Charles Bannerman, the first man to score a century in Test
cricket.

'First, I'd save my brother Alec, then Murdoch, then you, Spoff.'

'What about the Victorians?'

'I'd let 'em drown.'

Though this story is probably apocryphal, it captures the feelings between the States – feelings that were no less strong in Miller's day, with 'renegades' particularly suspect. Miller was at a disadvantage because he was preferring the personally more congenial state to the political heavyweight. Victoria effectively controlled Australian cricket, and years later when Miller was a strong contender for the national captaincy the move and its attendant circumstances were among the factors that told against him. Yet the move can also be seen as the completion of the process started by the war. He was now an international cricketer with a certain pronounced reputation. Sydney matched his mood and his personality. It provided the necessary cosmopolitan background.

The distance between Sydney and Melbourne is only just over 400 miles and the air flights almost as regular as a bus service, yet the difference in attitude and physical make-up is enormous. Melbourne has a more limited, less beautiful setting. Its character is more provincial, its customs and attitude more formal. Even during the forties, Melbourne was governed by a strict élite. Invitations were printed and posted in the best Mayfair traditions of the 1920s; there were garden parties and tennis gatherings straight out of Somerset Maugham, the Melbourne Cup provided the ladies with a chance to rival Ascot and the Lord's Day Observance Society exercised a tremendous influence. In Melbourne on a Sunday there would be no newspaper, no cinemas, no organised sports.

Nothing could have provided a greater contrast than Sydney. Physical beauty apart – the harbour, the bridge, Bondi Beach (Miller still spends many happy hours on the Sydney beaches) – there was its distinct and diverse multi-national atmosphere with immigrants from every central European country, its claim to be the cultural centre of Australia, its convincing air of licentiousness. Only in Sydney was it possible to circumvent the severe drinking laws that closed bars at six in the evening. The gambit was simple: order drinks with a meal before six and as long as the meal lasted drinks were constantly replenished.

Then there were the Sydney girls. In a male-oriented society all Australia seemed aware of them. Sir Neville Cardus always claimed that he only had to see the walk of women of the two cities to be able to distinguish them. While the Melbourne woman had a certain strait-laced, virginal inhibition, the Sydney ones seemed challengingly free.

Miller developed an instant rapport with Sydney. Whenever he walked into the Randwick racecourse bookies would lengthen the odds, shouting, 'So-and-so 6 to 4 now Keith Miller is here', and Sydney soon became his favourite cricket ground. He had always found the vast amphitheatre of Melbourne suffocating: 'When playing there I always feel like an early Christian thrown to the lions'. But the Sydney ground, with its magnificent setting, was more inviting: 'The soft couch grass makes it feel as if you are playing on a carpet'. Also, there was the Hill and there was Jack Perryman. Perryman was no Yabba (the legendary Australian barracker) but he was to become Miller's most public fan. He was reported never to have missed a single Miller match and every time Miller played he was ready with his endearments. They rarely varied: 'Keithie, you champ-pee-an, I love you, Keithie', and every Christmas there was a card from 'your old mate on Paddington Hill'.

Miller at Sydney was an almost certain draw. As he came out to bat, Hillites would nudge one another, spectators sleeping in their shirt sleeves would be awakened, little boys would whistle and cheer and the ladies in the Sheridan stand would sit up. 'Miller's in'. He never let his admirers down, and some of his greatest Australian deeds were performed at Sydney.

The life-style defined, he developed one of his most memorable friendships. He met Neville Cardus, predictably in a bar:

I was having a quiet drink, Keith was engaged in an argument with someone about some innings of his: how many sixes he had hit, where it had been played. This person did not know he was arguing with Keith. He had a bet and said, 'Let's go to the newspaper office to check up the facts.' Then Keith revealed his identity. I was struck by the whole thing.

Cardus was in the middle of his Australian sojourn and for a time he and Miller lived in the same block of Sydney flats. Miller would often drop in and request some music. It was always the same: a piano concerto. Cardus and Miller comparing musical notes became a familiar scene at Sydney cricket parties, Miller would whistle a few bars of music and Cardus would have to identify it. Ray Robinson recorded one such moment:
Cardus, usually unerring, once replied, 'That's a Rossini overture, Keith.'
'No, Neville, listen again.' (More whistling).
'That's a Rossini overture.'
'No, Neville, that's from Beethoven's "Eroica".'
'But Keith, you are whistling up with the violins. That piece comes down with the cellos.'
He had entered Cardus's life at just the right time. Cardus was getting tired of the modern game. Within a few years he was to give up regular cricket writing in disgust. Miller was a throwback to the world Cardus treasured, the world of A. C. McLaren and Victor Trumper, 'a world capable of wonder, a world unstaled by too much achievement, by too much abnormal skill cultivated by neglect of imagination and relish of risk'.
Once Cardus was resignedly waiting outside his flat for some transport to take him to the Sydney Cricket Ground. Suddenly a taxi emerged, Miller leaned out of the window and shouted, 'Get in'. He had been to a party, was already overdue at the ground and had a splitting headache. 'I'm afraid you'll not get a great deal of brilliance before lunch, but I'll try and make up for it.'
New South Wales won the toss. Miller, having consumed innumerable pills, batted before lunch. 'He hardly played a ball. It was all Arthur Morris. But then after lunch, his hair

polished and shining, he played wonderfully, all gay and cavalier.'

Cardus would not hear a word said against Miller. I repeated to him some criticisms that had been made about Miller: arrogant, prima donna.

'Keith arrogant? No, never, never', and the passion in his voice seemed to obliterate the weight of his eighty-five years.

Miller's first season with new South Wales, 1947-48, could not quite match his astounding excellence of the previous year, yet he batted very consistently to finish second in the State averages: 392 runs for an average of 49. There was also one remarkable innings. With a marvellous sense of timing he hit 170 against the Sheffield Shield virgins and eventual champions, Western Australia. Opening the innings he made his runs in only three hours – his century coming in 88 minutes – hitting two sixes: one was a straight drive that ranked among the biggest hits seen on the Sydney ground and the other landed, to the great delight of the ladies, on the top deck of their stand. He also took five wickets in the match. It was Western Australia's only defeat of the season. His bowling was numerically prodigious: 143.2 overs were evidence that he was not being used just as a shock bowler, and his average of fifteen wickets at 36 runs each showed the strain.

The tourists that year were India on their first visit to Australia. They were without Merchant and Modi, two of their most reliable batsmen, both of whom had made huge scores against the Australian Services team, and before the tour began the Indians declared that they hoped Bradman would play, if only to allow them to learn from him. Bradman was happy to oblige. He averaged 178 and outside the Tests reached his hundredth hundred in first-class cricket, in the company of Miller. There was some speculation that Miller might steal the show but he unselfishly gave up strike to enable Bradman to reach the target, he himself making 86.

The Test Matches made no great demands on him, or for that matter on the Australian team, whose all-round superiority proved too much for the Indians: they lost four out of the five Tests, three of them by an innings. It was the type of cricket that had little appeal for Miller, the ritual slaughter of the weak by the strong: apart from the Second Test, when Australia were caught on a sticky wicket, he would come in to bat no. 5 after Barnes, Morris, Bradman and Hassett had reduced the bowlers to despair. In the First Test he made 58 brilliant runs, and in the Fourth a nonchalant 67. He was sparingly used as a bowler: his longest spell was twenty overs in the Third Test, his most remarkable the one in the Fourth Test when he took two wickets for six runs. He took nine wickets in the series. Eight of them belonged to the top half of the batting, including Hazare, the leading Indian batsman.

Already two problems were evident: the conflicting demands of batting and bowling, and disagreements with Bradman. Miller had set his heart on becoming a great batsman. Batting is the great glory of the game. Success is more pleasurably and immediately measured in runs and Alec Bedser's wry joke probably sums up the plight of bowlers: 'The last bowler to be knighted was Francis Drake'. Miller never concealed his dislike for bowling – surely no other great fast bowler has ever been so disinclined to bowl – and his career was punctuated by announcements that he had, or was about to, quit fast bowling. At the end of the Services tour he had publicly declared his preference. 'I do not want to jeopardise my batting career just to thunder away as a fast bowler.' Though, he qualified, he would not mind going on as a change bowler if required at any time. At the beginning of the 1946-47 season this was re-emphasised. He wanted to play against England but not primarily as a bowler.

Persuaded to open the bowling with Lindwall (O'Reilly tried to dissuade him), the effects of being an essential part of Australia's attack were beginning to tell. Ray Robinson observed:

His labours as one of the chief bowlers prevented him from approaching his batting with a fresh mind and untapped energy. The flame of his batsmanship was not burning with the same purity. The power was still there – he could hit as distant a six as ever – but he was tending to become a swash-buckling on-side hitter instead of a distinguished batsman with unrivalled hitting capacity as one of his qualities. The feet, ankles, shins, knees and thighs of such uncommon batsmen as Miller are among cricket's rarest possessions, far too precious to be tarnished and squandered in the dust and potholes of the bowling crease.

Robinson, like most other people who participated in this argument, was judging Miller by his 1945 form. This was a cross Miller the batsman was always to bear. No cricketer could have consistently reproduced that brilliance; no cricketer in the history of the game has.

Miller was never able to strike the right balance and even today there is no unanimity about the superiority of the rival skills. Generally the Australians favour his batting, the English his bowling.

His disagreements with Bradman were minor but revealing. During the Adelaide Test Miller, after a longish spell on a hot day, was enjoying a drink. Taxis were waiting to take the team to their hotel but he was reluctant to leave and soon there developed a row with the Secretary of the Australian Board of Control. The inevitable report followed. Bradman summoned him to his stockbroker's office. Miller describes his thoughts as he walked from his hotel to Bradman's office: 'Here I am just back from the war, a war which has been dangerous for me in parts, and I am sent for like an erring schoolboy called to the Head's study'. The summons did not amount to much, but the memory remained.

Both problems were to find dramatic focus during the 1948 English tour.

6

Miller had looked forward to the 1948 tour. It marked his return to the world of Dusty, the world of his old Air Force friends who would supply him with hoarded chewing gum, provide tips for horses and dogs, and expect tickets for matches. But he was no longer a completely free agent. He was now on official business, which began on the high seas signing autographs in readiness for the tour and continued with a series of set functions, though he did manage to get time off and attend race meetings in Paris.

England presented familiar problems: the war scars were still there and rationing was very much in force. In the Australians' opening match at Worcester a spectator remarked, as he saw the groundsman sprinkling sawdust in order to cover the bowlers' wet run-ups, ''Ere, go easy with yon sawdust. Why, yon man is wasting full month's ration of ruddy sausage meat.'

The serious business of cricket began appropriately with wind and rain at Worcester. Miller came in ninth, with the Australians comfortably ahead, and made 50 not out, hitting three sixes.

In the next match at Leicester, when the first Australian batsman was out, necks were craned to observe Bradman's arrival at the wicket. Hundreds of girls, men and women raced to the pavilion gate and cameras were cocked ready to click. But it was Miller who emerged, bowed in mock appreciation and the crowds scattered with a disappointed 'Oh'. Their disappointment did not last long. On a cold, Arctic day, he soon involved the crowds. One of his hits bounced into the crowd and sent a youth to the local hospital for the weekend, while another youth suffered a more significant conversion: Peter Smith had gone to the match proud of his off-spinning virtues, 'possibly county standard'. He watched the innings in a mixture of incredulity and fascination: this was personal fantasy come true. He left convinced of Miller's greatness, and was to spend hours trying to imitate his hero. He forgot off-spinning and concentrated on quick bowling and batting like Miller. He soon realised that he did not have his model's skills and decided to become a writer.

The innings revealed Miller's strategic sense and the range and mastery of his strokes. While he made 202 not out, only two other batsmen made over 30 – Barnes 78 and Bradman 81. On an easy Leicester wicket, as the early batsmen fell to the spin of their fellow Australians, Jackson and Walsh, he was stern; with Bradman he was experimental; and finally, when the tail required protection, he was mature and responsible.

The next match against Yorkshire – the closest the Australians came to being beaten – saw him in a different rôle. On a drying wicket he switched to medium pace off-spinners and took six for 42 and three for 49 and with Johnston won a very low scoring match. His 34 was the highest and most assured innings and included two sixes.

Then came the match against Essex. It remains a unique moment in modern cricket. The Australians won the toss and made 721 runs in a day, the highest ever made in a single day's play. Bradman, Saggers, Loxton and Brown all made centuries – the distinguishing feature being their rate of progress which varied from just under a run a minute to a run in a minute and a half. Miller came in to bat when the score was 364 for 2; he took guard perfunctorily and to the very first ball that was bowled to him he lifted his bat, flung his hair back and was walking towards the pavilion even before the bails hit the ground.

If ever a single situation could be said to epitomise the man, then this was it. Runs were there to be had, the Australians were to score another 357, but the idea had no appeal for him. As he walked towards the pavilion Bradman, the non-striker, whose instincts must have been outraged by the gesture, said to Trevor Bailey, the bowler, 'He'll learn'. Miller, as we shall see, didn't.

Nor did he regain his batting zest. Challenges were fast disappearing and there were increasing bowling demands made on him. On only two further occasions were the Australians in danger of defeat: Miller made decisive runs in both of them. Against Hampshire, the only county to head the Australians on the first innings and on a difficult Southampton wicket, he made 39 out of 117, hitting Knott, the most successful Hampshire bowler, for three sixes. Then in the second innings he took five for 25 in twelve overs, effectively deciding the match.

And, of course, he could not resist Lord's. MCC v. the Australians: in those days it was a curtain-raiser for the Tests with the best of the English batting ranged against the probable Australian Test side. Miller made 163, going from 91 to 100 in three successive balls and hitting three sixes – one of them was, to quote Cardus, 'one great blow square from the shoulders to the upper and non-alcoholic regions of the Tavern'.

This, his sixth innings of the tour, was to be his last three-figure innings, and his aggregate of 449 nearly half his eventual total for the tour. He did not reach his 1,000 till August and when his team-mates cheered he shaped up for the next ball with an inverted bat. The balance between batting and bowling, already disturbed in favour of bowling – at the end of the MCC match he had bowled 119 overs, 42 more than Lindwall – was to be completely compromised during the First Test. The stage was set for the bowler.

In English cricket memory the summer of 1948 will always have a special, horrifying appeal. It will be remembered as the summer Lindwall and Miller devastated the English batting, taking 40 of the 91 English wickets taken by Australia in the Tests. This was the season they entered the ranks of the immortals and set standards which would always be the ones to beat. If they had never bowled again, memories alone would have secured them a prominent place in history.

Yet as a pair they were to be really devastating in only one Test, the final one at the Oval; injury and circumstances conspired to limit them. In the First Test Lindwall injured his groin after thirteen overs and did not bowl again; Miller did not bowl in the Second and the first innings of the Third; the second innings of the Third, curtailed by rain, developed into a private war between Miller–Lindwall and Edrich–Washbrook; and the Fourth was played on a wicket that progressively aided spin. It remains a matter of conjecture as to what they might have achieved had they bowled more consistently throughout the summer.

Lindwall easily dominated the partnership. He took twenty-seven wickets at a cost of 19 each and twice took five wickets in an innings, effectively deciding the match. Miller took thirteen wickets at a cost of 23 each and his major individual contribution came in the First Test, where in the rain of Nottingham and on a wicket not particularly biased towards pace he proved himself to be a match-winning bowler in his own right. Statistically Bill Johnston was Miller's superior in that match: he took nine for 183 runs while Miller took seven for 163. Yet Miller's wickets comprised Hutton, Laker and Compton (twice each) and Washbrook (once). Laker apart (and he was the highest scorer in the first innings), these were batsmen who could decide a match.

It was Miller's duels with Compton that produced some of the most memorable cricket of the summer, what Cardus has called 'a match within a match': two of the most evocative cricketers of their age, or any age, ranged against one another. These duels belong to the great romantic legends of the game. They seemed to embody the hopes and frustrations of an entire generation, these clashes between players of the highest possible class that totally involved the crowd yet served to enhance their own personal friendship. This was only right: their characters were complementary, their wider public appeal coincided.

They were both all-round sportsmen of distinction, both able to amuse a crowd as well as enrage it, both forceful extroverts who could win matches with a single, decisive intervention – or fail gloriously – and both men's men, though the nature of their sexual appeal probably differed. Miller's was more primitive, and his tanned figure satisfied every English myth of the Australian male; Compton's was more comforting, and mothers of unmarried daughters must have felt a bit like Jane Austen's Mrs Bingley. Some twenty years later, in Melbourne, a lady came up to E. W. Swanton and said, 'My word, Mr Compton, but you have put on weight since your playing days'. Compton was genuinely amused when he heard the story.

In an age when international cricketers did not socialise to the extent they do now (that at least is Trevor Bailey's firm conviction: 'After all you would expect, say, Keith Boyce to know Keith Fletcher fairly well, they play in the same team for six months of the year'), the Miller–Compton friendship was widely advertised. Miller's third son is named Denis and Miller was the natural leader of the group that formed round him and Compton: Edrich, Lindwall and Evans. On and off the field they defined a life-style that immediately reduced their contemporaries to the ranks of the hoi polloi.

On the field in the middle of the most unrelenting battle there would be humour and a natural, easy give and take. The 1950–51 series was to produce some fairly unexciting cricket. It was during one such spell in one of the Melbourne tests that Evans reached 49. The crowd was dozing peacefully in the sun and Miller had been bowling for some time without effect. Suddenly he produced a bouncer. It was high, wasteful, innocuous. Evans waved an airy bat at it, the crowd roared, and Miller was stimulated. He shouted, 'Give me that bloody ball', marched towards the bowling mark, stopped after a few yards, abruptly wheeled round and produced in quick and identical succession (Evans recalls) 'two of the most beautiful bouncers I have ever faced. I could do nothing.' At the end of the over he reassured Evans, 'Sorry, Godfrey, had to liven things up.'

The group never carried their battles into the dressing room. At Old Trafford in the Third Test of the 1948 series a Lindwall bouncer hit Compton on the forehead. He was led away bleeding and came back to make 145 not out – one of his greatest innings ever. Rain often held up play during this Test and Godfrey Evans recalls one such occasion. 'We were playing poker and a pile of money had gathered, about £30 or £40. Suddenly the umpires went out. Keith said, "whoever has an ace wins", dealt the cards, held up an ace, grabbed the money and walked onto the field. And almost immediately he bowled some terrific bumpers at Bill'.

It is a life-style that does not appear to have survived their departure. A few years ago Compton went to the Middlesex dressing room. Middlesex, after a bad run, had just chalked up a win and Compton suggested a celebratory drink. He was genuinely surprised at the orders; even beer was excluded. 'Why, one chap even ordered a glass of milk.'

But the Miller–Compton similarities should not be exaggerated. Technically, Miller was the classicist, Compton the great improviser. Compton's sweep, played at times from outside the off-stump, became one of those inimitable strokes that in memory will always be associated with his play. Miller made no such innovatory contribution. Also Compton was, and this appears even more so in retrospect, a heroic, lonely figure: Horatius defending the bridge. For much of his playing career, Compton played in struggling English sides, and throughout 1948 he waged a lonely battle against the Australians. Miller for the most part played in strong Australian sides. His contributions were important, but they were not exclusive.

Their duels dominated international cricket for ten years but the First Test at Nottingham in 1948 epitomised these contests. It also provoked one of the most substantial crowd reactions of Miller's career. On the first day he had been politely booed for bowling bouncers at Compton. On the third day, a Saturday, the reaction was more pronounced. At that stage England could only hope to save the match. The Australian advantage was overwhelming: 509 to England's 165 and 39 for two with the major English pair, Hutton and Compton together.

Miller began by bowling off-breaks. Compton hit him for

four. Miller's reaction was immediate – he bowled a bouncer. This was his way of indicating, as Fingleton says, 'that his dander was up'. Right through his career he would react thus: clap his hands, demand the ball and bowl a bouncer. And though the wicket was placid a Miller bouncer commanded respect, induced hasty and erroneous judgements. It also conjured up for the Nottingham crowd a powerful memory: Harold Larwood. Trent Bridge in 1948 vividly remembered Larwood, the history of the bodyline controversy and the effect it had on his career – premature retirement. So in addition to national distress caused by England's performance, local wounds were re-opened by Miller's bouncers. At the beginning he was able to appease the crowd, tossing his hair back, laughingly indicating what he would do with a bouncer. But as the bouncers continued his every gesture was suspect: fielding to his own bowling and then running round and delivering the next ball in one continuous movement enraged rather than amused.

The explosion came in the last over of the day. He bowled three bouncers at Hutton (making five in eight balls), one of which struck him on the arm. As the Australian players came off an angry crowd pressed towards the pavilion; there were angry members inside. Miller was the last one in. There was suspicion about the crowd's ultimate intentions and suspense about his reactions. As he was about to enter the pavilion, a particularly loud member caught his eye. He was small, squat, neatly dressed and Miller lifted him and shook him, smiling all the time.

The man, rattled, blurted innocence. 'It wasn't me, Mr Miller. I didn't say anything.'

Miller laughed, put his man down and peace returned to Trent Bridge. Sir Douglas McCraith, Chairman of the Nottinghamshire Committee, apologised to Bradman, and on Monday the Nottingham Secretary broadcast a public appeal. Off the field there was peace, on the field the duels were resumed.

Miller soon bowled Hutton but Compton batted on into the fifth day before another bouncer dealt with him. He tried a hook, decided to withdraw when already committed and with the ball near his head, overbalanced and fell onto his stumps. The dismissal, clumsy and comical as it looked, was a commentary on Miller's pace on a fifth-day wicket. Don Tallon for one was convinced that it was the fastest ball Miller bowled on the tour. See plate 3.

Once again he had made the decisive breakthrough. Compton's innings of 184, commonly considered one of his finest ever, had provided hope and nearly produced security for England. Compton was sixth out at ten minutes to one; at twenty minutes past two England were all out and Australia easily made the 98 required for victory.

But the price was heavy. Miller had bowled 63 overs – 44 of them in the second innings – and he began complaining of a stitch-like pain in his left side. The Australians played two matches before the Second Test at Lord's and he played a very minor rôle in one of them. By the time the Second Test arrived his pain was acute, and there was to be a far-reaching sequel.

Australia won the toss and made a very laboured 350, Miller making 4 before falling to Bedser. England began their reply before lunch on the second day. Lindwall bowled the first over, then as Miller was about to take his place in the slips Bradman tossed the ball to him. Miller tossed it back. To the observers, and it was a packed Lord's with gates closed before the start of play, it was a sensation. Soon stories were circulating of how Miller, the 'prima donna', had refused to bowl for Bradman; how he had 'indulged in histrionics', fielding a ball in Lindwall's first over and then clutching his back and complaining, 'Oh, my back'. His explanation, as recorded by Bill Edrich, was simple:

> In the dressing room, just before going on to the ground that morning, I had told Bradman I was not fit enough to bowl. He agreed with me and said he would ask Bill Johnston to open the bowling. I was astonished when he threw the ball at me.

Bill Edrich, who was padded up to go in no. 3, believes that had Bradman asked Miller again there might have been a stand-up row in the middle of Lord's. Bradman called on Bill

Johnston and Miller did not bowl again – one over against Surrey apart – till the second innings of the Third Test.

Miller had every reason to be unhappy about the technical use made of him. In his first four innings he had made 236, twice not out, and the 1,000 in May appeared a reasonable speculation. His next match was against Cambridge. He was listed sixth but while his colleagues made 414 he did not bat and was the major Australian bowler. Progressively, as we have seen, the bowling demands increased, and by the end of the tour he had bowled 138 overs in Tests and 429 in all matches.

In Bradman's scheme of things Miller the batsman was expendable. The team was excellently served by its batsmen. Morris, Barnes, Bradman and Harvey all averaged more than 66 runs in the Tests, Bradman, Hassett and Morris more than 71 runs on the tour; and there were forty-seven hundreds. Also, the accent that season was on pace. Under an experimental law the new ball was available after every fifty-five overs. Bradman needed two of his opening bowlers always to be fresh and with Toshack often unfit, Miller had to share the burden with Lindwall and Johnston.

It is possible that Bradman had a less than exalted opinion of Miller's batting. Gubby Allen told me: 'The Don and I don't agree on a lot of things. But on one thing we are agreed. Keith was no better than no. 6 in a good batting side'. I say possible because Bradman, understandably, would not commit himself over the telephone and did not reply to my letter.

The technical problems only served to highlight the deep and fundamental differences in temperament and outlook and, given these differences, it would have been surprising if the two had not clashed. It would be easy for a biographer of Miller to present Bradman as an ogre. Like no other cricketer before or since, he made the game his business. He was by deliberate choice, and perhaps by upbringing, a loner. There are many stories told about his skill, his brilliance, his courage, but there is none that reveals humour. As Robertson-Glasgow wrote: 'No one ever laughed about Bradman. He was no laughing matter.'

But the apportionment of moral blame is less than useless. No two modern cricketers could have been more dissimilar in outlook, upbringing and basic instincts. Bradman had followed a cricket path completely different to Miller's and the war was to be another crucial divide. Bradman had never been through a war (too young for the first, unfit for the second). Miller, as we have seen was always acutely aware of his operational experience. It was inevitable that the two men should have spoken with such conflicting tongues.

Sir Neville Cardus illustrated these differences well.

In a Test match at Sydney, Keith was on his way to the wicket when a little boy approached him for an autograph. Keith waved aside the disapproving guardian of the law and signed his autograph. What would the Don have done in his place? He would have said, 'Naw (and Cardus successfully imitated an Australian accent), 'that would disturb my concentration'. But can you imagine how happy that little boy must have been?

In 1948 there were other factors. Bradman, unlike previous tours, was first among equals rather than all-powerful; Miller's popularity was a strong and rival centre of attraction. And Bradman had set himself one last ambition: to lead an unbeaten side through an English summer. Only one other team had ever attempted it, Warwick Armstrong's 1921 side. But Armstrong had failed in the last match arranged as a special challenge by the former Lancashire and England captain, A. C. MacLaren. Bradman had read his history and in 1948 every match was played extra hard and festival matches were specially suspect. Miller did not hide his annoyance.

In early August the Australians returned to Old Trafford for Cyril Washbrook's benefit match. Jack Ikin, who had been having a lean spell, had just reached 99 for the second time in successive matches when the new ball became due. Six minutes of play remained, the match was already a draw. Bradman took the new ball and handed it to Miller. Miller said, 'Give it to Sammy', a reference to Loxton, one of the friendlier medium-pacers. Bradman turned to Lindwall who, having fewer scruples about such things, promptly bowled Ikin, still one short of his century.

For the festival matches Bradman stipulated the maximum permissible number of England Test players and often played his strongest teams. In the Scarborough festival match – the last match of the season – the Australians faced, probably, the strongest side outside the Tests and Bradman treated it as a full-scale Test Match. Miller told Jim Laker: 'Don't think we're all as prim as this little man, Jim. I want no part of it. This is no way to play festival cricket and I'm ----- if I'm going to support this "head down" idea. I don't care if I don't score a run.' He scored a single, then gave his wicket away.

Miller also found irritating Bradman's habit of projecting the image that everything was meticulously planned. At the Oval Test Compton hooked a Lindwall bouncer but could not keep it down and Morris at short square leg took the catch. Bradman rushed up to Morris and said: 'Well caught, Arthur. You know why I put you there now. I remembered he played that shot in 1938.'

The clashes were to leave their mark. Miller and the Australian cricket authorities were always to be at loggerheads – Bradman was, is, Mr Cricket in Australia – and at the end of the following Australian season there was to be a sensational sequel.

As if to emphasise the liberating effect of not being Australia's no. 1 bowler after Johnston had opened the bowling instead of him at Lord's, Miller now played two of his best innings of the series: 74 in the second innings at Lord's, 58 at Leeds. Given Australia's superiority – 431 ahead with seven wickets in hand – his Lord's innings was welcome though not decisive; in terms of spectator appeal it was one of the best of the season. He came in to bat just as the Lord's crowd, resigned to a grim England struggle, had been awakened by two wickets in successive deliveries. Virtually the whole of Lord's appealed as Yardley rapped him first ball. He survived, and a few moments later hit one of his sixes just behind square and half-way up to the grandstand. Fingleton wrote:

This is a beautiful stroke of Miller's. As all know who have tried it, such a stroke requires the very essence of split-timing, as unlike a stroke down the pitch, the bat must pick the ball up at one very precise spot. Miller hits across the ball and up at the same time to get elevation.

A batsman with a reputation for hitting sixes always causes a stir. It generates a primitive excitement, and in a game that can often be indecisive it produces a clear conscious moment of decision, of violent affirmation of action. In Miller's case his physique, his approach to the game, his reputation all combined to make the spectators duck instinctively as he shaped to make one of his hits. There was another factor about his hits to leg. They were struck with great power from the left arm, so much so that in the follow-through the right hand would disengage, giving the impression of a one-handed shot. On a dull, damp day at Swansea towards the end of this tour, he was to hit Watkins, the Glamorgan opening bowler, with his left hand only, and leave Fingleton gasping, 'The most amazing batting feat I have ever seen . . . This was positively an unbelievable stroke'.

Lord's had been an exercise in public relations. Once, Miller lunged at Laker, missed, Evans searched for the ball, Miller directed him towards the sky. All the while the ball lay at Evans's feet. The Fourth Test at Leeds was more serious. It also inspired probably the most significant innings of his career. England had come to Leeds looking for a win. 2-0 down, they had to win if the rubber was to be shared. The omens were favourable. England had had much the better of the drawn Third Test and Barnes, one of the most successful Australian batsmen, was injured. England began well and made 496, their most substantial score of the series.

Then, on the morning of the third day, Pollard in three balls removed Bradman and Hassett. 68 for 3. Bradman's Australia faced its gravest crisis. Miller (who had faced just one ball and hit a three) was joined by Neil Harvey playing his first Test innings. Then, in the words of Arlott, 'for an hour and a half Miller played like an emperor'. In that time Miller and Harvey put on 121 runs, Miller making 58 of them.

This was the quintessential innings of that phase of his

career: peerless strokes, strategical vision, crowd involvement, violence. Miller drove Pollard from the attack (in ten overs he conceded 40 runs) and reduced Bedser to a toiling busybody. On came Laker, immediately Harvey was morally 'out' and Miller got Harvey away from the strike. He hit Laker's first ball to him for six and drove him repeatedly through the covers. And, of course, he could not forget the crowd: he amused them, he frightened them. Miller tried to drive Laker. Laker, sensing it, dropped short. Miller adjusted hurriedly but safely, jammed down hard, tossed his hair back and laughed. The crowd laughed. A few balls later Miller hit Laker over the long-on boundary and into the crowd. A blonde girl was led away limping.

Now Harvey was secure. He hit Laker for three fours in one over and went on to make his reputation with a century in 177 minutes. By then Miller was out, at 189, and Australia were out of immediate danger. Even his dismissal is worth recording. It came after he had hit Yardley for two fours. Yardley sent his men deep, bowled his next ball wide outside the leg stump. Miller, desperate to hit a six, overbalanced, fell and just managed to touch the ball with the bottom edge of his bat. The ball hit Evans on the head and Edrich, diving full length, held the ball with the tips of his fingers. Earlier in the day the crowd, who were overflowing on to the ground, had paid respectful homage to Bradman. Now they feverishly applauded Miller. Fingleton recorded the scene:

> I retain a vivid mental picture of Miller as he walked back that sunny Leeds day. When he is embarrassed by the applause, his eyes sweep the sky as if searching for Nazi planes. He tossed back his hair with a jerk of his head, he plucked his shirt over his chest with his left hand and with the right he waggled his bat aloft to the crowd in appreciation of their appreciation. And then a tall, dark, handsome figure in his white flannels, he disappeared from view down the slapping, clapping lane with his police escort. This was an innings, this was a moment to live in the cricket memory.

John Arlott concluded:

Every stroke would have been memorable but that each ousted
its predecessor from the appreciation. Miller's was not merely a
great innings but I cannot believe it possible for a cricket brain to
conceive of any innings which could be greater.

The Australian recovery continued – it finally reached 458
– but Miller saw little of it. Still in his cricket boots and
flannels, he was on an adjoining Rugby League ground
instructing several thousand spectators in the art of drop-
kicking from the half-way line.

Leeds had also seen the proper resumption of the
Lindwall–Miller partnership. On a wicket where the lack of
an extra spinner – slow left-armer Jack Young was left out –
conceivably cost England the match and Australia made 404
to win in the fourth innings, Lindwall and Miller were the
major Australian bowlers. Miller's back had recovered
sufficiently for him to bowl 38 overs, Lindwall bowled 64
overs, and between them they took a third of the wickets that
fell.

Three weeks later came the Oval Test. Yardley won the
toss, batted, Miller and Lindwall bowled through the
sawdust. Within two and a half hours England were all out for
52, their lowest score against Australia in England. Miller
made the initial breakthrough by bowling Dewes. At
Cambridge, earlier in the season, Dewes had batted with
towels wrapped round his body which made him pro-
nouncedly rotund. He had strong memories of the Victory
Series when Miller had hit him in the same vulnerable place
thrice. But towels did not help him at Cambridge – he made 6
before being bowled by Miller – and at the Oval, sans towels,
he made 1. Miller took one more wicket, that of Crapp.
Lindwall, substantially, did the rest. In eight overs after lunch
he took five wickets at the cost of 8 runs. At the end of the
innings Lindwall, in sixteen overs, had taken six for 20;
Miller, in eight overs, two for 5. Hutton with 30 had been the
only obstacle. It marked the most complete mastery of the
pair. Never again were they to be so dominant, nor English
batsmen so inept. Even the fall of wickets has a certain ring
about it:

1	2	3	4	5	6	7	8	9	10
2	10	17	23	35	42	45	45	47	52

That Saturday, Walter Robins, a selector, was playing at Dover. As the scores came in, Brian Valentine, the Kent skipper, sent a telegram to Holmes, another selector: 'Robins has shot himself'. It was, happily, an exaggeration but one which effectively summed up the national mood.

The Australian reply was dominated by Morris while Bradman, in his last Test innings, made his now famous duck and Miller 5.

The English second innings was a more protracted affair – 188 – and for a change Lindwall secured the wicket of Dewes. Miller had Hutton caught by Tallon for 64, the highest English score, and he bowled Crapp. Earlier he had hit him in the middle of the skull with a ball that rose suddenly; Crapp's resulting headache was still with him when he caught the Bristol Express the following afternoon. This time the Australian wickets were more evenly spread with Johnston taking four, Lindwall three and Miller two, as Australia won by an innings and 49 runs. As the crowds bade farewell to Bradman and sang 'For he's a jolly good fellow', Miller made a small boy happy. In the inevitable scramble for souvenirs Miller took a bail and tossed it high and wide. A small boy in front of the Press Box grabbed it gratefully.

He finished the tour with 1,088 runs for an average of 47.30 and fifty-six wickets at a cost of 17.58 each – the best all-round Australian figures since Charlie Macartney's 1926 tour. He had also taken twenty catches, eight of them in Tests, most of them in the slips, almost all of them vital. In the First Test he caught Hardstaff balancing himself on his spine (see plate 6); in the Second Test he caught Compton (he was to catch him four times in the series) diving forward from slip and ending up on his knees. It was the second ball of the fifth day, Compton was 29 and looked capable of saving England. With his departure England collapsed swiftly.

But Miller raised such high expectations, such abnormal hopes, that contemporary opinion was not completely satisfied. *Wisden,* out of 'reluctant necessity', did not name him as one of the five cricketers of the year. Hassett, Morris, Tallon, Johnston and Lindwall superseded him. Though *Wisden* was appreciative of his skills, it felt that 'he did not live up to his reputation as the finest all-rounder in the world'. Robertson–Glasgow wrote: 'But almost from the first he seemed mis-cast and out of joint. His daring deteriorated to profligacy. Excitability took the place of fervour.'

Not that it worried him. He was always able to divorce cricket from his wider interests and an English tour provided plenty of opportunities for the latter. Towards the end of the tour the Australians were shown round Windsor Castle and Miller met Lord Tedder, whom he had admired since his Air Force days. Tedder came up to him with a full tea tray and said, 'Excuse me, Sir, your tea.' Miller contained his surprise and said, 'Thank you, boy', and gave him a penny as a tip. Tedder tipped his cap in acknowledgement. Miller was touched as well as amused by the incident.

By now Miller was an established celebrity and though still unable to look the crowd in the eye, particularly in his moments of glory as at Leeds, he was very conscious of his image. He carried a soft, silk netting comb in his pocket. It fitted neatly over his fingers and he had become so adept at its use that what appeared as a casual wave was an effective combing of his hair – always the most distinctive part of his person.

He had also achieved an unusual distinction. He was mentioned in the 1948 Debrett. During the season one of his strokes had been described as 'being out of Debrett' and the editor, C. F. J. Hankinson, wrote: 'Debrett has long been a term to denote the superlative, but we cannot recall its having been applied to a game on any previous occasion.'

7

The 1948-49 Australian season promised to be one of peace and nostalgia. It was the first purely domestic season since the war and Bradman was playing his farewell matches. It was to end in one of the bitterest controversies in Australian cricket with Miller very much the central character.

He had returned from England with a great many aches and pains and he played right through the season under various pressures. He played several matches with a swollen shin, his wife was expecting a child and in between cricket he was flat-hunting and settling down to cricket journalism with the Associated Newspapers of Sydney.

Miller began the season well. In the opening match against Queensland he made 109 and in the next match against Western Australia he made 52 and took two wickets for 22 – the wickets of the Western Australian openers. Then as the pressures mounted he fell away: in four successive innings he made 0, 12, 6 and 26. But in the return match against Queensland, batting with only one clear eye – he was suffering from acute conjunctivitis – he made 52 not out after New South Wales had collapsed to 28 for 5. It was the highest score of the innings and it decisively turned the match. He followed this with 99 in the vital match against Victoria, an innings widely considered to be one of the best of the season and one that laid the foundation for a narrow New South Wales victory.

He finished third in the State's batting with 363 runs for an average of 45.37. He had not bowled a great deal. In 62 overs he had taken nine wickets for an average of 22. Once again he had declared that he wanted to be considered as a batsman, and even as just a batsman, there was very little to choose between his record and those of Harvey and Loxton. Friends, unhappy about his repeated generosity to inferior bowlers, were not particularly worried. The Australians were due to visit South Africa and that promised to be an easy tour.

Then came the first of two Australian farewell matches to Don Bradman, played before 41,000 Sydneysiders (the second was on 4-8 March 1949 at Adelaide). In the previous English season, the Australians had played the Gentlemen at Lord's with Walter Robins, a personal friend of Bradman, playing his first official game against the Australians since the war. Robins, a selector, had been critical of the way the English batsmen had played the bouncer and the Australians decided to provide him with an opportunity to demonstrate. Miller's first ball was a bouncer; it nearly decapitated Robins and considerably amused Bradman. Miller was intrigued. How would Bradman react to his bouncers?

That sunny Sydney afternoon Bradman had made 49 in less than an hour when Miller was brought back to bowl. His first bouncer was a fairly mild, harmless one and Bradman hooked it for four. Even as the crowds acclaimed Bradman's fifty, Miller was clapping his hands, demanding the ball and striding back to his bowling mark with that particular toss of his head which could mean only one thing: bouncers. Bradman had no answer to the first, the second he hooked, but the man who never lifted the hook stroke could not quite keep this one down, and he was caught. The crowd were incensed, Miller triumphant. A few days later Bradman and his co-selectors announced the team to tour South Africa and an astonished cricket world learnt that Miller had not been selected.

The day the team was announced Miller was at the Cricketers Club in Sydney. Chappie Dwyer, one of the selectors, was having a drink with Hassett. Normally he would have greeted Miller but on this day he ignored him. Miller understood. As Alan Barnes, the secretary, put up the team on the notice board he saw Miller looking over his shoulder. 'Ah, well, I expected it,' said Miller.

The decision provoked a furious reaction. Fingleton called

it 'one of the worst selection blunders in Australia's cricketing history'. Ray Robinson wrote: 'I thought it was the ugliest blot that had splashed from the pen of the selectors on to the pages of Test history.' And E. W. Swanton felt that Miller's omission was for reasons 'other than technical'. A cartoon in the Sydney *Sunday Sun*'s news review *Fact* showed and MCC member telling another in the Long Room: 'Fancy, Miller and Molotov in one week'. (Molotov, the long-serving Russian Foreign Secretary, had recently lost out in the post-Stalinist power struggle and had been dismissed.)

Two Sydney citizens fought in the street and were fined.

Miller prepared to settle down to a season of exclusively domestic cricket in 1949-50 and gave serious thought to quitting the game. Then news came from South Africa. Bill Johnston, who was to prove accident-prone, had injured himself in a car accident. Would Miller care to join the party? The injury to Johnston was not serious enough to prevent him from becoming the leading Australian wicket-taker in Tests, but the South Africans were insistent and the Australians keen to bury the controversy. Urged by his wife, Miller accepted.

The South Africans were not particularly strong. Their record since the war was dismal. Athol Rowan, their gifted off-spinner, was injured and did not play in any of the Tests, and their leading batsmen, Eric Rowan and Dudley Nourse, were nearing forty. The Australians were to win four of the five Tests, three of them by wide margins, and in only one Test were they really extended.

Miller had a good tour – not an outstanding one, but a good one. He was easily the leading all-rounder in either side. In Tests he took seventeen wickets for an average of 23 and made 246 runs for an average of 41; on the tour he took forty-four wickets for an average of 16.54 and made 577 runs for an average of 38.46. As in England, the bowler dominated the batsman. In the Tests he bowled 135 overs, only 25 less than Bill Johnston (the leading wicket-taker) and his bowling was decisive in two Tests in almost identical circumstances.

In the First, at Johannesburg, after Australia had made 413 he took five for 40 in fifteen overs in the first innings and virtually decided the match: Australia won by an innings. In the fifth, after Australia had made 549, Miller took four for 42 in fourteen overs in the first innings: Australia won by an innings.

As a bowler he had also acquired a new rôle: stock bowling. In the Third Test, which probably provided the best cricket, South Africa won the toss, and made 240 for 2 on the first day. There was overnight rain and Hassett, who had succeeded Bradman as Australia's captain, was determined to avoid batting on a tricky wicket. He told Miller and Johnston to impart no spin to the ball, set his field in completely defensive positions and South Africa crawled to 311 all out. Miller in twenty-four overs took one for 73, Johnston in thirty-one took four for 75. Though at the end of the day Australia were all out for 75 Hassett had won time. The weekend intervened, South Africa were bowled out for 99 and Australia won by five wickets through a brilliant century by Harvey.

The series also marked the first man-made interruption to the Lindwall–Miller partnership. In only one Test – the Third – did they open the bowling. Generally Lindwall opened with Johnston and Miller came on as third, fourth or even fifth change. And in the Fifth Test, for the first time in his career, Lindwall was dropped. He finished with twelve wickets and by the end of the series serious doubts were being expressed about his future.

As a batsman Miller consolidated rather than initiated. He generally batted no. 3. This was Bradman's old position and for much of Miller's later career it was to be Harvey's, who had an outstandingly successful South African tour. When the openers, Morris and Moroney, made runs, Miller responded with productive efforts: 58 in the first innings of the Second Test after a 68-run stand; 84 in the first innings of the Fourth Test after a 214-run stand.

His best batting came outside the Tests. Against Eastern Province, on a damp Port Elizabeth wicket, he made 131 with six sixes and seven fours; one of the sixes cleared the grandstand and landed in a pond. This almost rivalled his other huge hit during the tour. In an innings of 24 against North-

Eastern Transvaal at Pretoria Miller hit a six which cleared the trees and landed in the nearby Rapies river. A local reporter was so carried away that he got the name wrong and suggested a river eighteen miles away – not even Miller could hit that far!

But Miller's most memorable moments of the tour were spent in the State of Natal. In the country match he took six for 24; twice he appealed for lbw, twice the umpire wearing a hat with a wide drooping rim refused. Miller lifted the droop, bowled again, appealed and was successful. He restored the droop. And in the State match at Pietermaritzburg, while he was making 56 and taking six for 35, Peggy Miller gave birth to their second son. The child did not stand a chance: he was named Peter after the town.

Personally, the tour was an enjoyable one. Hassett was a popular skipper, he had a delightfully impish sense of humour and Miller easily renewed his old associations with him. Also, race consciousness was not yet a factor, the South African way of life was yet to come under severe scrutiny, and there were plenty of occasions to indulge in what was becoming a growing pastime for cricketers: golf.

Once Miller was playing golf with Alan Walker, his New South Wales fast bowling colleague, and Lindwall. Walker hit a shot into the bushes and went to retrieve the ball. Suddenly there was a scream. Walker emerged holding the leg of his trouser. 'Keith, Keith, there's a snake up my leg, he's bitten me, I've got hold of it. What'll I do now?'

Just behind them was a ladies' four-ball. Miller glanced at them and suggested to Walker that he take off his trousers. At that time talk of the black mamba was fairly common and Miller and Lindwall waited, golf clubs raised, to strike at the deadly snake. Walker took off his trousers; out wriggled a lizard some six inches long. Miller gravely offered both the lizard and the trousers to the ladies.

8

Miller began the 1950-51 season in absolute glory. In the opening match against Queensland he made 201, hitting five sixes. Ten days later in the return match at Sydney he made 63 in the first innings. In the second innings New South Wales were left 131 minutes in which to get 225. Opening the innings with Morris, Miller made 78 and New South Wales won by ten wickets with eleven minutes to spare. Three days later MCC were playing on the same ground. Miller began tentatively – he was very nearly bowled first ball by Bedser and Wright troubled him – but then he settled down and the character of the match changed. With Morris he put on 265 for the second wicket, Miller making 214, Morris 168. While Morris was partial to the cross-bat shot, Miller displayed his rich repertoire. Anything pitched up was driven, anything short was cut, sometimes delicately late cut, and he hit three sixes. The one off Hollies did not rise very high yet landed thirty yards beyond the sight screen.

It was during this innings that Compton, who was captaining MCC, went up to Hutton and asked for his advice. He replied, 'I'd send home for another bowler'. Compton's selection as vice-captain to Freddie Brown had appeared to indicate the selectors' preference between the two rivals. He was to have a miserable series – average 7 – did not do particularly well as an understudy and the next time Australia played England, Hutton was captain.

At this stage of the season Miller had made 616 runs in six innings, twice not out, for an average of 154. Four days after the MCC match, he played against Victoria, caught his bat in his pad and made a duck. A week later, with less excuse, he made another duck, against South Australia. But outside the Tests, this represented an interruption: in two games against the MCC he made 62, 98 and 1, and at the end of the season he easily headed the Sheffield Shield batting with an aggregate of 607 and an average of 121.

It is tempting to see Miller's career as forming a single continuous pattern of cavalier bursts interspersed with long spells of inactivity – tempting but wrong, unfair. It is not so much that the pattern is wrong – he was never one to apply himself day in and day out – but the cavalier bursts cannot and should not be equated. The Miller of 1950-51 was not the Miller of 1945. E. W. Swanton noticed a change during the New South Wales–MCC match: 'His demeanour seemed noticeably calmer than that of the mettlesome fellow of the last two Test series.' And after his innings of 99 in the Fourth Test A. G. Moyes wrote: 'Miller was the mellowed, matured master, able in these days to concentrate and withstand temptations which a year or two ago would have caused him to throw away his wicket.'

By the end of the series critics, English as well as Australian, were almost unanimous in endorsing this appraisal of the 'new' Miller. The essence of the cricketer or the man did not change. He was still supreme in his ability to involve a crowd to provoke its anger one minute then in the next, with a placatory wave of his hand or a toss of his hair, to move it to laughter. He still had no rivals as an interventionist: in a couple of overs he could shape a whole match. But Miller the batsman was reacting to changed circumstances.

It is possible, as some have suggested, that this was the result of the South African controversy; more likely, there were very valid cricket reasons. Without Bradman Australia found runs difficult and Miller was called upon to rescue rather than consolidate. Leg-theory or 'in-coming' form of attack had begun to inhibit his stroke-play. Cricket was moving into a new age, the age of defensiveness, now dignified by the term 'professionalism'. Inferior sides were now sustained by shrewd captaincy, team-work and, to borrow a term from another discipline, maximisation of scarce resources. Leg-theory – medium-pacers swinging or cutting the ball on or about the leg stump to a well-populated leg-side field – were its main technical weapon.

Recently on a wet Birmingham Test day I sat talking to Jim Kilburn of the *Yorkshire Post*. Kilburn is not particularly enamoured of the moderns, which is understandable. His heroes were conceived in the classical age. But as the talk turned to Peter May a glow came into his eyes. 'If he had stayed in cricket for another couple of years we would have seen the end of this sort of stuff [leg-theory]. He would have finished it with that superb shot of his wide of mid-on'. That remains debatable. May played it – one of the most difficult shots in the game – with a relaxed ease that seemed to indicate second nature. Yet to effect changes in a whole way of life more than mere technical skill is required: there is the crucial test of character. This is amply illustrated in Miller's case. His technical skills were never questioned, yet he rarely evoked the thoughts like those of Jim Kilburn about Peter May. He could seize and reconstruct a game, perhaps a series, never an age. He never thought that far ahead.

For the rest of his career Miller learned to coexist uneasily with this form of cricket, but there was a characteristic touch: the contest was individualised. A man emerged to personify the mood and the period – Trevor Bailey. The Miller–Bailey duels have none of the qualities of his other contests. There was very little brilliant cricket, hardly any romance and no enlivening wit. They were part of the prolonged and bitter war between the Cavaliers and the Roundheads, a war that is still part of cricket and perhaps always will be.

In the winter of 1950-51 the war began badly for Miller. Then came Sydney. At that stage he had made 15, 8, 18, 14 in his first four Test innings, out to Bailey (twice), Wright and Brown. Miller the serious bowler had virtually disappeared. He had not bowled at all in the MCC match against New South Wales, and had had seventeen overs in the First Test for three wickets. He displayed a wide variety of styles and poses for the Australian XI in their match against the MCC, including one round-arm ball, bowled almost from the waist, which had Reg Simpson lbw. In the Second Test, which was also the first time in the season that Miller had opened with Lindwall, he had bowled eighteen overs for two wickets.

For their part, England – 0-2 down – had arrived in Sydney for the Third Test desperately seeking a win and confident of success. The team that had left England the previous autumn with no more, it seemed, than a gutsy leader and some willing workers had exposed the weakness of the Australians: only ninety-eight runs was the total of the two defeats. So, on the eve of the match, all England oozed confidence. All that was required was a good start and some luck, then the Australians could be beaten – so the theory ran.

On a hot, cloudless Sydney day England began well. There was an interruption. At 34 Washbrook lashed at Johnston, Miller at second slip anticipated, dived to his right and took the catch one-handed – it was to become his favourite catch. Soon Hutton and Simpson assumed complete command and with the wicket placid and the Australian attack innocuous, a sizeable score was a reasonable speculation. All this while Miller had been fielding on the boundary, communing with the ladies in the Sheridan Stand. Then, with the new ball soon to become due, Hassett decided to call on him for a warm-up spell.

It was to prove electrifying. His third ball forced Hutton to hurry and had him lbw for 62. Three balls later Compton was late on one that pitched outside the off-stump and dragged it on to his stumps. Sheer pace had done it – see plate 4. Miller was bowling faster now that in his opening spell and Parkhouse survived to tea without indicating stability. Soon after tea, in Miller's third over, Simpson, trying to push one away to leg, deflected it into short-leg's hand. England had slumped to 137 for four and Miller had taken three wickets for 5 runs in 3.7 overs – all with the old ball.

This was to be the decisive moment of the Test match and the series. Brown, Bailey and Evans tried in their various ways to retrieve the situation but the advantage was lost. Next day England were all out for 290, Miller finishing with four for 37. He might well have run through England that particular afternoon, he had looked in such total command, but for a curious decision by Hassett: when the new ball was taken he gave it to Johnston and Lindwall.

By the time Miller came in to bat, with Australia 122 for 3, progress had been so slow that the English attack was looking quite formidable. Four hours and ten minutes later, at the end of the day's play, he was 96 not out, having hit only three fours. It was very much a 1950–51 Miller innings: wickets fell around him, for periods he did not have the strike and he had to contend with leg-theory, particularly from Warr, with six men in defensive positions on the leg-side. And Warr was no slouch.

He had gone out to bat promising fireworks and as he came in he met Neville Cardus. Cardus remonstrated, 'What happened to all the gay, cavalier stuff you promised me?'

Miller replied, 'I was under orders. The wicket is taking spin and Hassett wants a big lead before he lets Iverson loose. But wait till you see me tomorrow.'

The next day he went from 100 to 145 in an hour, and hit a huge six into the M. A. Noble Stand. Australia finished with 426. When England batted he bowled six overs, Lindwall four, then Iverson came on, took six for 27 in nineteen overs and England were beaten by an innings between lunch and the close of play. Australia had retained the Ashes.

This innings of Keith Miller's provoked a great many theories. They all centred on his ultra-defensive 96 and they all indicate the hold he exercised over his contemporaries and still does. Some suggested that he was being chivalrous. England were without two of their principal bowlers, Bailey and Wright, and he did not want to humiliate an injured side. O'Reilly was angry because sections of the Press seemed to be applying double standards. Hassett who had also played a slow innings was criticised, Miller was praised. Recently a leading cricket writer, whose measured prose never fails to soothe me, told me: 'It was one of the most boring innings I have ever seen. It completely disproves the idea that Keith did not care for runs'. Then he checked himself: 'I don't think I would like to be quoted on that' – this twenty-seven years

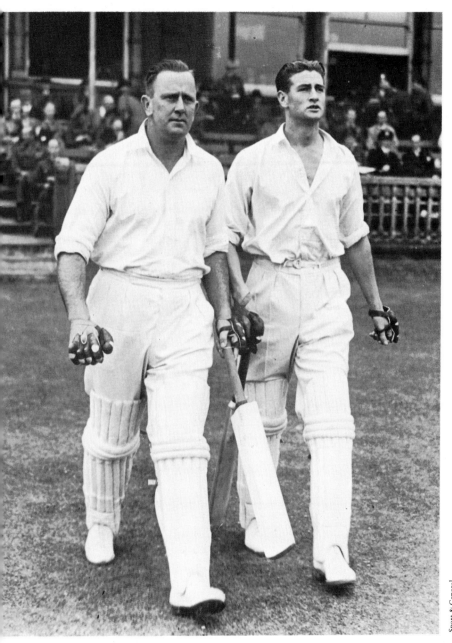

1. Keith Miller goes out to bat with Cec Pepper in the Fourth Victory
Match at Lord's in 1945.

Sport & General

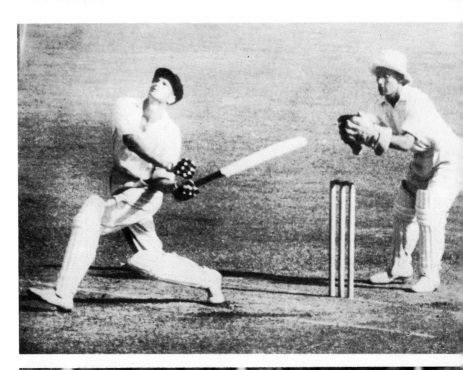

2. Miller the batsman. *Above,* a six off Wright in the First Test at Brisbane
in 1946-47, while Gibb appears to be pleading for mercy. *Below,* in the first
match of the 1948 tour against Worcestershire.

Sydney Morning Herald   Sydney Morning Herald   Press Association

Central Press

3. Miller the bowler. *Above,* the superbly balanced action, which enabled
him to disguise variations of pace. *Below,* the effect at the other end of the
wicket: in the First Test of the 1948 series at Trent Bridge, Compton
misjudges a hook against a Miller bouncer and falls on his stumps (see
page 62).

4. An over which changed a series. In the first innings of the Third Test of the 1950-51 series, at Sydney, Miller has Hutton lbw for 62 (*above*) and three balls later bowls Compton for a duck (*below*). England had reached 137 for 1 wicket before Hutton's dismissal and looked as though they might establish a dominating position for the first time in the series. They were all out for 290 and Australia won the match and the rubber (see page 79).

Fox Photos

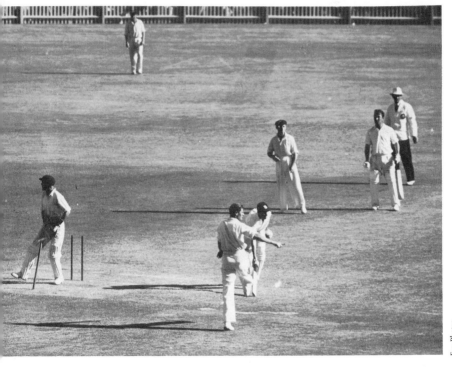

Fox Photos

5. Two incidents from the 1950-51 series. *Above,* Miller (fourth from left) collects his usual souvenir of a stump at the end of the Australian victory at Brisbane in the First Test. *Below,* Gilbert Parkhouse is run out in the second innings of the Third Test and Miller appears to be pre-dating Tony Greig by some twenty years by pointing to the pavilion!

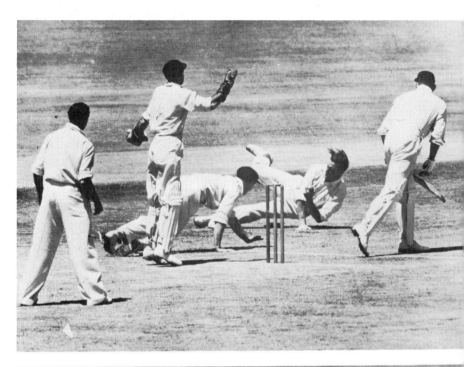

6. Miller the fielder. *Above,* during the Fourth Test at Adelaide of the 1950-51 series, he appears to catch Freddie Brown off his first ball: everybody on the field, including Brown, thought he was out, but Miller at once indicated that he had taken the ball on the half-volley. *Below,* no mistake, despite the acrobatics, with this chance from Hardstaff off Johnston in the Nottingham Test of the 1948 series.

7. The 1951–52 series against West Indies, with Miller at slip supporting his partner, Lindwall. *Left,* Rae, the West Indian opener, is bowled by the third ball of the First Test at Brisbane. *Below,* one of the shots in the 'bumper war' which was a feature of the series: Stollmeyer is felled by a short ball from Lindwall during the Second Test at Sydney.

Fox Photos

Fox Photos

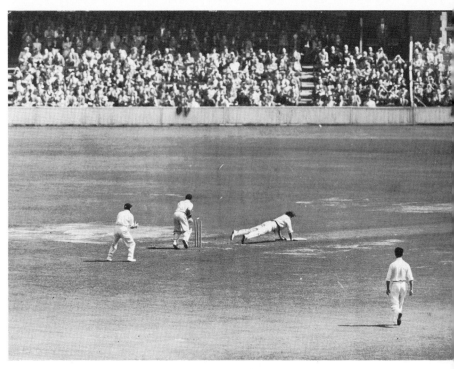

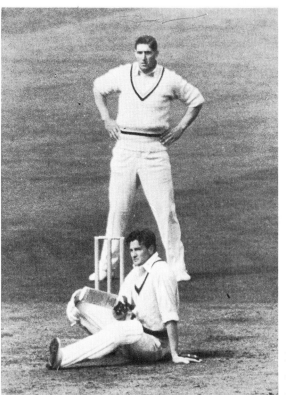

8. Miller the unorthodox. His unique batting style sometimes landed him in un-cricketer-like positions, particularly against the spin bowlers. *Above,* he is stumped by Godfrey Evans off Hollies in the Final Test of the 1948 series in England. *Left,* he appears not to be amused by the results of this shot against Yorkshire in 1953.

Press Association

9. Off the field. *Above,* dressed to kill: with Ray Lindwall on ss *Orcades* as they prepare to hit England in 1953. *Below,* entertaining royalty during the 1953 tour while Lindsay Hassett listens appreciatively.

Sport & General

Press Association

10. All-rounders' duel. *Above,* Miller bowls to Bailey during the Oval Test in 1953 while a young Freddie Trueman backs up. *Below,* Bailey has Miller lbw for 1 in the same match.

Central Press

Fox Photos

11(a). Is it imagination or does Miller look a little disillusioned as he walks out for the first match of the 1956 tour to England behind Ian Johnson? It had been widely expected that Miller would lead the party, but Johnson's appointment ended Miller's last hopes of captaining his country.

Sport & General

11(b). Miller caught by Oakman during the historic Fourth Test at Old Trafford in 1956 – one of Laker's nineteen victims in the match.

12(a). Miller's farewell to Test cricket as he is applauded to the crease by the England side in the Fifth Test of the 1956 series at the Oval.

12(b). Old adversaries in harness: Keith Miller and Len Hutton playing together for MCC against Ireland at Lord's in 1959.

after Miller had played the innings. Miller was so precious that any deviation from the image – however slight – had to be justified.

After the Third Test Miller, helped by injuries to Bailey, began to enjoy his cricket a great deal more. In the Fourth he hit 44 and 99 and after being bowled by Wright he cheerfully presented his bail to the first schoolboy he saw in the grandstand. He also took three wickets for 3 runs in three overs to conclude the match – another Australian victory by 274 runs. In the Fifth Test, Miller and Lindwall produced their best bowling of the series. On the afternoon of the third day England were 204 for 2 in reply to Australia's 217. Then in half an hour on a Melbourne wicket that gained in pace all day as the sun beat on it England were reduced to 217 for 6, Lindwall taking the wickets of Compton and Brown, Miller the wickets of Sheppard and Evans. But for the first time in their careers the intervention failed to be decisive. Simpson made 156, the Australians fell to Bedser and Wright – Miller making 7 and 0 – and, cheered on by a crowd that genuinely sympathised with the valiant efforts of Brown and his men, England gained an eight-wicket victory, their first over Australia since the war.

The series had once again emphasised, if emphasis was needed, Miller's worth to the Australian cause. He was top of the batting with 350 runs for an average of 43.75, and the dominant partner of the Lindwall–Miller partnership – seventeen wickets at a cost of 18 runs each while Lindwall took fifteen wickets at a cost of 23 runs each. In fact, the partnership was at a slight ebb: they had rarely bowled together and, apart from the Fifth Test, not very well. For the first time in his career Lindwall had gone through a series without taking five or more wickets in an innings, always a measure of bowling dominance.

The season also provided Miller with one moment of supreme personal satisfaction. At thirty, Victoria's slow bowler, Jack Iverson, had become the great freak success of the season. His unusual grip and prodigious spin had mystified both English and Australian batsmen and by the end of the season he was to head the Test averages with twenty-one wickets. A duel between him and the New South Wales batsmen was eagerly anticipated. At Melbourne in the first match Miller, Morris and Burke were out before Iverson came on. But at Sydney in January, soon after Iverson's great victory over England in the Third Test, Miller, Moroney and Morris hit over 300 runs, Miller making a spectacular 83. In twenty overs Iverson conceded 108 runs. It was to be a decisive moment in his career. He did not play in the following Australian season, and just at the beginning of 1952-53, with an English tour in the offing, he suddenly withdrew from the Test trial against New South Wales. Jack Hill took his place both for the State and for the 1953 English tour and Iverson never played for Australia again.

So by the end of the 1950-51 season the Roundheads could feel some satisfaction. The Cavalier had been curbed, but there was still a lot of life left in him. There had been persistent newspaper reports that he had been selected as a Labour party candidate for the middle-class Sydney suburb of Burwood in a by-election to the New South Wales Parliament. Miller had denied the rumours but his postbags had come to bulge with advice and for a time friends began to call him Disraeli.

Already he was a legend. In the Prime Minister's room in Parliament House in Canberra there hung two pictures. One was a landscape by Tom Roberts, one of the founders of the Australian impressionist school, the other was a photograph of Keith Miller finishing a cover-drive. It was said that in moments of acute political stress Mr Menzies (later Sir Robert) would look at the photograph and be reminded of the glory of ancient Athens.

9

Some time before the start of the 1952-53 season Miller travelled to Hong Kong to play a week's festival cricket. It was in a bar of this unlikely cricket centre that he was to hear perhaps the most surprising and delightful news of his entire career. He was relaxing with a few other cricketers when a man approached him. 'You are Keith Miller, aren't you? They've just made you captain of New South Wales.'

Miller was staggered. In the previous season, 1951-52, Arthur Morris had led New South Wales to the Sheffield Shield, he had averaged 127 with the bat and Miller had had his most anonymous Shield season. In six innings he had made 192 runs with a highest score of 57 and an average of 32; he had taken four wickets at a cost of 55 runs each. But the man in the bar was sure, he had a newspaper and Miller slowly recovered from the shock. While he was thrilled by the challenge, he felt sorry for the way his friend Arthur Morris had been treated.

Perhaps Miller should have felt a premonition, for it had been a strange trip. On the flight out from Darwin Miller was sitting next to Bill O'Reilly. Suddenly O'Reilly said, 'Keith, there is something wrong with one of the engines'.

Miller, his pilot's ear all attention, listened hard. He detected nothing and dismissed O'Reilly's fears. A few minutes later the engine went dead and the plane had to return to Darwin.

On closer examination, Miller's elevation to the captaincy was not all that surprising a decision. At the start of the 1952-53 season nothing was right with Australian cricket. Bradman had gone and the crowds had gone with him. Tennis was now the most popular game and crowds were no longer prepared to sit and wait for the rare cricket thrill to appear. New South Wales, despite winning the Shield, had lost £6,000. It had also lost out in the quarrel between the States, always a feature of Australian cricket. Dwyer, a prominent New South Wales administrator and a selector for many years, failed to get re-elected and the State which was the major playing force in Australian cricket found itself without a voice at the national level. Sydney seethed with anger. There was talk of secession and several reprisal plans were discussed, though in the end nothing tangible materialised. These feelings were to be further aggravated during the 1952–53 season when the team to play South Africa in the First Test at Brisbane was chosen. Announced just after New South Wales had beaten Victoria, it contained six from Victoria, four from New South Wales, none from Queensland. The Brisbane crowd, angered by the rejection of its idol Tallon, was so vociferous in its support of the South Africans that the Australians felt that they were playing away from home.

Miller was Sydney's answer and for a time Australia's – he was also named vice-captain to Hassett for the South African Tests. Though his Shield performances were poor – but then the Shield rarely provided an indication of his true form – the previous season, 1951-52, had once again emphasised his stature. At the end of that season's Test series John Goddard, the visiting West Indian captain, had echoed the sentiments expressed by nearly every captain since the war: Miller's had been the decisive influence on the series.

During Miller's playing career no other series excited the same degree of world-wide interest as this first post-war series between Australia and the West Indies. Consumer recovery had just begun, and the history of recent Tests had lent to the series that instantly understood title, World Cricket Championship. Newspaper correspondents came from all over the world and even Alec Bedser wrote a book as an interested neutral.

The West Indians were justifiably expectant. They had just won the 1951 series in England by the overwhelming margin of 3-1 and Freddie Brown's team had hinted at the frailness of the Australians: batting prone to disaster, bowling that could be contained. The West Indian resources appeared sufficient. The three W's – Weekes, Worrell and Walcott – brought up on hard, true wickets, would know how to deal with Lindwall and Miller, and the spinners, Ramadhin and Valentine, would completely nonplus the batsmen.

The Australians were most concerned about Ramadhin, who had become a legend in the course of one season. He had started the English summer of 1950 as an unknown twenty-year-old Trinidadian and ended it with 135 wickets and a great many baffled English batsmen. Morris and Barnes motored up to Newcastle – a hundred miles from Sydney – to watch him in the first match. They learned nothing. Ramadhin was still a mystery. All they had was Compton's description of him (to Miller): 'All you see is a blur of black hand, a white shirt with sleeves buttoned down to the wrist and a red ball.'

Miller first met Ramadhin just before lunch on the second day of the First Test. The West Indies, after being hustled out for 216 by the pace of Lindwall (four for 62), Johnston (two for 49), and Miller (one for 40), had struck back swiftly. When he came in Australia were 80 for 3. Four runs later Harvey was out. Valentine had taken three wickets, Ramadhin one. The inexperienced Hole and Lindwall apart, there were no recognised batsmen left, and on the soft Brisbane turf Ramadhin was getting a lot of purchase for that most mysterious of his weapons, the leg-break.

Miller's form till that point had not been exactly inspiring and Ramadhin had mimicked his tendency to reach forward. But his reaction to the first ball he received reassured the crowd. He swung at it, missed, overbalanced and fell with a thump. He laughed. The crowd laughed. Miller was in the right mood.

The first ball Ramadhin bowled to him was swept for four, and he hit another before lunch. The first ball after lunch was bowled by Valentine and Miller drove it back over his head for a six. Ramadhin did trouble him but he was enjoying his innings and keeping both the crowd and the West Indians amused. He would miss a sweep then wave his bat at the fieldsman to indicate where the ball would have gone, run a quick single and poke Walcott, the wicket-keeper, in mock indignation at the sharp fielding, or if Ramadhin's spin deceived him he would indicate to the adoring crowd more deadly ways of imparting his own spin. In print this may read like cheap histrionics, in practice it was part of Miller's ability to lighten a mood even when the going was serious and the match the First Test of a series meant to decide the unofficial world cricket champions.

Then Lindwall joined him and in thirty-eight minutes the pair put on 59. Lindwall was boisterous, he was also lucky and five catches were dropped in half an hour. Lindwall finished with 61, Miller with 46, and Ramadhin took one for 75 in twenty-four overs.

But this represented a check, no more. In the second innings he took five for 90 and only some determined batting by Hole and Lindwall constructed a three-wicket Australian victory. The leg-break was still a mystery.

Three weeks later the two teams met at Sydney. Again the Australians were in trouble. Hassett had won the toss and, on a wicket affected by rain-water which had seeped under the covers, asked the West Indians to bat. They responded with 362, their most substantial score of the series. Australia were 106 for 3 when Miller joined Hassett. Now came the decisive duel with Ramadhin. While Hassett in his quiet, undemonstrative fashion played mainly on the back foot, Miller was most effective when using his long reach and in five hours the pair had put on 235 runs, breaking Bradman's and Ponsford's 21-year-old record. The mystery was solved. Miller could now detect the leg-break and Ramadhin had to place three fieldsmen on the leg boundary to try and contain him. He was finally out for 129, Hassett for 132; Australia finished with 517 and at the end of the innings Ramadhin's figures read 41–7–143–0. He was never again to exercise any significant influence on the Australians. The course of the series was set and the calypso crowds had to compose a new song:

Ram called Hassett a rabbit
But the Indian boy he regret it.
Ram bowled seriously,
But he was bowled to the boundary.
Hassett made a century
And Miller followed immediately.

Then Miller helped Lindwall and Johnston convert a possible victory into a certainty. This was the Test where the 'bumper tactics', which by the end of the series were to provoke such bitter anger, began, though only one wicket fell to a genuine bouncer: Rae to Miller. He took two other wickets – Christiani and Walcott – to finish with three for 50; Lindwall took two for 59 – Worrell and Gomez – and Australia were left 137 to win. Miller, who had developed a knack of being in at the death, made the winning hit and collected his usual souvenir: a stump.

He did little in the Third Test, which provided the only West Indian win of the series, but as if rejuvenated he dominated both the Fourth and Fifth Tests. On the first day of the Fourth, in conditions that helped fast bowling – warm and sultry, a wicket with early life in it – he took five for 60 and with the help of Lindwall (one for 72) and Johnston (two for 59) bowled out the West Indians for 272. Then with Australia once again facing imminent collapse – three of his four major innings in the series were played under such circumstances – he had a crucial stand with Harvey.

While Harvey in an effort to regain form attacked, Miller, in his growing rôle as father figure, dropped anchor. Compare this with Leeds in 1948 when in similar circumstances both Harvey and Miller attacked; it indicates the increased responsibilities Hassett's team imposed on Miller. The pair carried Australia from 49 for 3 to 173, Miller making 35 to Harvey's 89, before Miller was finally out for 47 after batting for two and a half hours. It was one of his slowest innings ever, but its importance was quickly emphasised. After he was out six wickets fell for 43. In the second innings he took two crucial wickets (Stollmeyer and Christiani), each time removing a batsman who looked like converting resistance to rescue, and Australia eventually won the match through a thrilling 38-run last-wicket stand.

Miller always reserved his most characteristic performances for Sydney. For three-quarters of the first day of the Fifth Test he did not seem to be in the game at all. Gomez, one of the few West Indian successes of the tour, used the hot and humid conditions effectively to take seven for 55 and bowl out Australia for 116. In reply Lindwall and Johnston, opening the bowling, removed Rae, Stollmeyer and Walcott for 18. Then Miller came on. His first ball was delivered with a casual swing of the arm, almost a loosener. Christiani patted it back for an easy caught-and-bowled. In another seven overs Miller had bowled out the West Indians for 78 and his figures read 7.6 – 1 – 26 – 5. He followed this with an innings that was pure mood. In just under an hour he made 50. So complete was his dominance that while Hassett, who had reached his 50 by the time Miller came in, added 8, Miller made 38; and so great was his hold over Sydney emotions that even his clumsy moments like falling over backwards while attempting a sweep, or ending up cross-legged trying to hook, appeared witty.

Miller made most of his runs on the second day. On the third day he quickly went into the sixties, then in the last fifty minutes of his innings made 3. Mood. There is no other explanation for it. The bowling was the same that he had so exhilaratingly annihilated the previous evening and while he brooded, his partner – Hole – moved from 14 to 40.

Miller's interest revived sufficiently to help Lindwall bowl out the West Indians. Lindwall took five for 52, Miller two for 57, and Australia won by 202 runs.

So once again Australian pace had won the argument. Miller and Lindwall finished with forty-one of the eighty-seven West Indian wickets that fell to Australian bowlers (the two along with Johnston took sixty-four of the eighty-seven, none of the West Indian batsmen averaged more than 36 and Ramadhin took fourteen wickets at a cost of 49 runs each. Miller himself was second to Hassett in the batting with 362 runs for an average of 40.22 and top of the bowling with twenty wickets at a cost of 20 runs each.

But it was not all joy. There had been growing unease about the 'bumping tactics' (the phrase is *Wisden's* used by Lindwall and Miller to curb the three W's. In the second innings of the Fifth Test, as Lindwall averaged two bumpers an over to an injured Weekes having earlier in the series bowled them at an injured Stollmeyer, this unease exploded into deep and bitter anger which was to have its repercussions in domestic cricket. That evening John Goddard told Fingleton and O'Reilly, 'We thought we were coming to Australia to play cricket'.

O'Reilly later told Fingleton how he had already tackled Lindwall: 'I saw Lindwall that same afternoon and I told him I thought his tactics bloody shocking, that he had made himself look cheap and that I had written so for the next morning's *Herald*'. For Lindwall this was cruel irony. Fingleton relates how just after the war Lindwall was playing for New South Wales, captained by O'Reilly, against Victoria:

> On the way from Adelaide to Melbourne, O'Reilly told Lindwall: 'I might have a few words to say to you when we get out on the field.' Tamblyn was opening for Victoria, and in the Woodfull manner he was a heavy scorer for his State. O'Reilly told Lindwall: 'I want you to bowl the first ball at Tamblyn's shoulders. He might do something silly.'
> Lindwall, amazed: 'What, the first ball?'
> O'Reilly: 'Yes, the very first ball.'
> Lindwall's eyes opened up but he did as he was told and we got Tamblyn out early. O'Reilly reported: 'Lindwall said to me, "He doesn't like a bouncer, does he?"'

On that January afternoon when O'Reilly rebuked Lindwall, Lindwall recalled history, 'Do you know who taught me to bowl the bouncer?'

O'Reilly was quick to reply, 'Yes, I did, but I will always be against it as you bowled it today and you can draw whatever analogy you like'.

If Lindwall appears to be singled out, this is not deliberate partiality. Miller was a most active collaborator in the general use of the bumper, but it was Lindwall's bumpers to an

injured Weekes after the series had already been decided that
provided the ultimate spark. Fingleton, looking back from the
singular vantage point of probably the most exciting and
warm-hearted Test series ever (the 1960-61 West Indies visit
to Australia) wrote:

> Our bouncers then were grossly overdone and it was a reflection
> upon our cricket that they were not stopped. As it was, instead of
> seeing three of the most brilliant batsmen of all time playing their
> strokes, we saw them repeatedly ducking to earth under the
> bouncers – about the most ungainly and uncricketlike sight in the
> game.

But not all the arguments were on the side of the angels.
The major West Indian batsmen had a reputation for being
fearsome hookers. In the First Test Weekes had dealt quite
comprehensively with Miller's bouncers and in the Fifth
Stollmeyer had scored a century. Also Miller's cricketing
instincts remained generous. In the Second Test he took a
'catch' offered by Christiani off Lindwall's bowling. Everybody was convinced it was a catch and a photograph later
confirmed this. But Miller signalled 'no catch'. It was
Christiani's first ball and he went on to make 76, the highest
score of the innings.

The reaction in domestic competition was perhaps
inevitable. Victoria had always resented New South Wales's
monopoly of pace and tried, ineffectually, to retaliate in a
Sheffield Shield match. The umpire warned some of the
bowlers and at the end of the season the New South Wales
Association suggested a change in the law which was accepted
by the national body. The alteration meant that umpires could
intervene whenever anybody bowled short, even if it was
directed at the stumps.

So the 1952-53 season began with an attempt to curb the
short ball and with Miller, as we have seen, captain of New
South Wales and vice-captain of Australia. He had inherited a
young team. Richie Benaud had just made his Test debut, the
previous season Ian Craig had been the youngest player to
appear in inter-state cricket, and under Miller Bobby

Simpson made his first-class debut at the age of sixteen. Miller was to make a singificant impression on these and other young players. Alan Davidson has written about his effect:

> I have always thought Miller's casual approach left a marked impression on Richie Benaud who developed a habit, too, of making last-minute arrivals at various grounds. Indeed, in these early days, Benaud unconsciously modelled himself on Miller. For instance, Richie always wore a cap in his early days, but later discarded it and in later years regularly played bare-headed.

Miller was to mould this team into one of the most successful New South Wales sides. In four seasons New South Wales won the Sheffield Shield three times, and the Miller school was to produce cricketers who were to dominate international cricket till well into the sixties. Yet the essentially casual approach remained. Once New South Wales played a one-day fixture at Maitland, near Newcastle. Maitland, then, was a small country town and the New South Wales team with its glittering array of stars merited a full-dress civic reception. The Mayor made a suitable speech, then Miller rose to reply. 'Mr Mayor, we're very pleased to be here in this town, er . . . this city . . . er . . . er . . . where the bloody hell are we anyway?'

Miller's first important match as captain of his State in 1952-53 was against the touring South African team in November. He won the toss, put the visitors in and his field placings caused Johnnie Moyes's spine to tingle and an onlooker to comment, 'Fancy placing that field to Bradman or McCabe': no third man, no fine leg and a ring of fieldsmen placed provocatively round the bat. But the South Africans had no Bradman or McCabe. They lost three wickets for three runs and were all out for 202, Lindwall taking five for 30. New South Wales, with the help of sound batting from Craig and skilful bowling by Benaud and Davidson, won by five wickets.

The return match, where Miller again put South Africa in, was notable for the way he encouraged youngsters. He dropped himself to no. 8 in the batting order, watched Craig, who was

immediately and disastrously likened to Bradman, make his
first century and helped him towards his second, while he
himself made 58 rather quietly.

Miller had already started the Sheffield Shield series with
victories in both the matches against Queensland. But the
most impressive performances were, naturally, reserved for
Victoria. On a Melbourne pitch that looked 'green' he sent
Victoria in. The gamble appeared to have failed when
Victoria made 347, Miller's four wickets costing 103 runs. But
though Miller made 16 – falling to Hill – Barnes made 152, de
Courcy 110. In the second innings Lindwall took two wickets,
Burke, an infrequent bowler, mopped up the tail and New
South Wales won by an innings.

At this point New South Wales were yet to be beaten and
were strong contenders for the Shield. Then came the match
against South Australia. There had been rain, no play was
possible on the first day, and when South Australia won the
toss New South Wales were asked to bat. Miller faced an
awkward choice. There was no Barnes and the pitch had
obviously been affected by rain. He decided to reverse his
batting order. He opened with Lindwall and Trueman, the
wicket-keeper, and sent Davidson in at the fall of the first
wicket – these three usually batted nos. 9, 11 and 10. On this
occasion Morris and Craig were sent in nos. 10 and 11.
Lindwall made 70 but only three others made double figures –
Miller himself 28 – and Noblet, the South Australian opening
bowler, with six for 39 bowled out New South Wales for 148.
Then, despite Miller's personal efforts – five for 35 in twelve
overs which restricted South Australia's first innings to 164,
and 71 in the New South Wales second innings – South
Australia won, thanks to hundreds by Favell and Hole.

It was the last match that Miller played for New South
Wales that season. Soon there were Test calls and then injury.
But his youngsters carried on the fight in the remaining three
games and it was not until early February in the return match
with South Australia that the Shield was finally lost with New
South Wales finishing second.

Miller's last Sheffield Shield match of the season was also

notable for a joke that was to have serious consequences on his career. Sid Barnes, making a strenuous comeback bid, was not selected to play in the First Test against South Africa. In the previous season his selection to play the West Indies had been vetoed by the Australian Board of Control on the implied grounds of misconduct (jumping a turnstile at Melbourne and taking movie pictures were two of the alleged misdemeanours). Barnes had cleared his name in a celebrated court case. Though this time the authorities did not disclose the reason for his non-selection, the feeling persisted that he was still subject to the backlash of accumulated 'sins'. Barnes was so angered by this decision that he stood down from the New South Wales side but volunteered to be twelfth man. He also decided to stage an act, informing Miller and Morris of his intentions. When drinks were called, Barnes accompanied the waiter. Dressed in a flunkey's uniform, he carried a brush, a comb, a vaporiser, a mirror, an iced towel, a cigar box with a few cigars and a radio; only time had prevented him from acquiring a top-hat. The act went well, Miller ordered a second drink, the waiter went to fetch it and Barnes posed in the middle. Though the Saturday crowd at the Adelaide Oval were diverted, the authorities were not amused. Barnes never played for Australia again, and when the team to tour England was announced Morris replaced Miller as vice-captain under Hassett. The incident itself was always brought forward as an example of Miller's inability to impose discipline.

For Miller the 1952-53 series with South Africa was marked by successes with the ball, batting problems against Tayfield, the South African off-spinner, and injury. The South Africans had begun under extremely adverse conditions: their record was uninspiring, they had no crowd-pulling players, they were expected to be a financial and cricketing disaster and some critics suggested that the series be cancelled. Yet, in one of the great upsets of post-war cricket, the series was tied 2-2.

The South African success was based on two factors: application in both batting and bowling and some grand fielding. Nowhere was this more evident than in the Miller–Tayfield duels.

These duels started the first time they met in early
November in the New South Wales–South Africa match.
Miller made 30 and 29 and fell to Tayfield both times; in six
Test innings he was out to Tayfield five times, averaging 25. It
is generally conceded that Tayfield was not a great spinner.
There was nothing intrinsic in his bowling that made him a
match-winner, which we may accept as a definition of a great
bowler. He bowled a good line and length, he was persistent
and – this is crucial – he was backed by some marvellous
fielding that converted steady bowling into match-winning
efforts. The South Africans took some spectacular catches,
including a memorable one by Tayfield himself, but the one
that dismissed Miller at Melbourne in the Second Test is
worth recording.

This was Miller's most satisfying innings of the series – 52,
which brought him his thousandth run in Test cricket – and
the only time he looked like mastering Tayfield. While his
colleagues were pinned down by the accuracy, Miller
produced some of the best driving of the season. Then, just as a
century looked inevitable, he lifted Tayfield towards the
long-on fence. The ball seemed certain to clear it when
Endean, his arms held aloft, suddenly plucked the ball from
the air. A. G. Moyes described it as 'one of the historic catches
of Melbourne or any other ground and which will become
part of cricket history'. Characteristically, Miller applauded
the catch.

He played one other innings of note. At Sydney in the Third
Test he made 55, putting on 169 for the third wicket with
Harvey. The partnership bettered Armstrong and Hill's
record set up in 1910-11 and firmly set Australia on the road to
victory. Again, Miller was out to Tayfield.

But not all his batting problems can be traced to Tayfield; a
great deal was self-inflicted. He appeared to have discarded
the cut, that most thrilling stroke in his armoury. In fact, he
seemed to be disenchanted with strokes behind the wicket and
seldom displayed them. Though his drives contained all their
old power, they unerringly went to hand. He often produced
thrilling strokes but he rarely converted them into an innings.

As a bowler Miller (and his partnership with Lindwall) was most productive in the lost Second Test and the victorious Third. In the Second he took four for 62 and three for 51, reaching a personal landmark by taking his hundredth Test wicket; Lindwall took three for 29 and two for 87. In the Third Lindwall took eight for 112 in the match and Miller five for 81.

Injury had dogged him right through the season. In the First Test a throat infection prevented him from bowling in the second innings. In the return New South Wales–South Africa match it was an infected toe. Then in the Fourth Test, after he had bowled just one ball in the third over, he stopped to pick up the ball, pulled a muscle in his back and collapsed. He did not play again that season and for the first time since his debut missed a Test. Lindwall was also injured in the same match – after bowling thirteen overs – and did not play in the Fifth Test. The absence of the pair was immediately felt. South Africa drew the Fourth from a losing position and won the Fifth after Australia had made 520 in the first innings. So, while the Australians prepared for England, there was deep anxiety. Was Miller really fit for an English tour? How long would the partnership survive? As the SS Orcades sluggishly wound its way towards England – its engines had broken down just off Melbourne and it arrived a day late – the doctors probed and tested Miller and Lindwall. They were satisfied.

And they were right. Miller and Lindwall were to play in four more series, but in the wider cricket sense the season marked the divide in the partnership. At the end of it their career figures read:

	Balls	Mdns	Runs	Wickets	Averages
Lindwall	7,186	165	2,689	132	20.37
Miller	6,109	148	2,194	107	20.50

As a pair they had reached the peak of their performances. In only one further series – in the Caribbean in 1955 – were they to prove collective match-winners but then they were costlier than usual: forty wickets at a cost of 32 runs each. They went on bowling together, they rarely destroyed together. In England in 1953 Lindwall was clearly dominant:

he took twenty-six Test wickets at a cost of 18 runs each while
Miller took ten wickets at a cost of 30 runs each and was being
written off as a fast bowler. In Australia in 1954-55, though
Lindwall was ahead on wickets, Miller's interventions were
more spectacular. Finally, in England in 1956, in conditions
that inhibited fast bowling, Miller took twenty-one wickets
at a cost of 22 runs each while Lindwall took seven at a cost of
34 runs each. Lindwall, of course, was to go on. He chased
Clarrie Grimmett's Australian Test record of 216 wickets,
secured it, then lost it fairly promptly to Benaud; many felt
that he stayed in cricket too long. But all that is not part of this
story. The Miller–Lindwall partnership is.

Pairs are perhaps the most evocative element of cricket.
They provide the necessary balance in a team game that
allows most unbridled personal glory. And there have been
some memorable ones. Pairs of great batsmen, of great
spinners, of great fast bowlers and some pairs like Hornby and
Barlow who are part of the folklore of the game. Statistics
could be quoted to determine relative merits, but that would
prove nothing. Each pair remains unique in its own manner
and its own particular moment of glory. It must be judged in
the conditions in which it operated and its effect on its
contemporaries. On both counts Lindwall and Miller stand
supreme.

Lindwall and Miller operated in an era of unprecedented
fast bowling shortage. Until 1952, when Trueman emerged,
none of their opponents had a fast bowler and it was not until
1954-55 that another pair – Statham and Tyson – threatened
their exclusive position. This meant that they could impose
their own standards on batsmen unused to pace and bowl
without any fear of retaliation. Yet this does not detract from
their achievements. They always sought and impressed class:
129 of Miller's 170 Test wickets belonged to the first seven in
the order, as did 137 of the 200 Test wickets Lindwall took
during Miller's career. And the batsmen they fought –
Hutton, Compton, May, Cowdrey, Worrell, Walcott,
Weekes and Hazare – would have held their own in any age.
Lindwall and Miller parleyed on slightly superior terms with

all of them; none of them ever mastered the pair. Their effect on opening batsmen – always the first test of fast bowling – was devastating and there were only eight century opening stands scored against them in Tests. Hutton and Washbrook were the most effective with five, Richardson and Cowdrey with two and the Indians, Mankad and Sarwate, one. The timings are interesting: six of these came in three series between 1946 and 1948, the last two in 1956.

Their dominance of the Australian attack was equally decisive. In every series of the ten years of their partnership they bowled between 30 per cent and 45 per cent of the overs and took between 30 per cent and 53 per cent of the wickets (the odd series at the beginning and end of their partnership apart). Of their eleven major series together, in only three did they fail as collective match-winners, and those were the only ones Australia lost. They came to exercise a tremendous psychological hold over their opponents. Every season preparations would be made to combat the 'terrible twins' and every season the Australians would express misgivings: Lindwall was not the same bowler, Miller did not want to open the bowling. Bill Johnston was a favourite stalking horse. But come the First Test at Brisbane, Lindwall would bowl a reassuring first over and Miller would follow.

They left a legacy: the Carmody or umbrella field. Sometime after the war, Miller, Carmody, Sismey and a few others sat drinking one day in a Shepherd Market pub. Somebody sketched the outlines, Carmody used it in the Sheffield Shield, and Lindwall and Miller got a reluctant Hassett to accept it. It was to become synonymous with their bowling and a sure indication of the Australian mood. With five slips, a gulley, a leg slip and two short legs, the batsman looking behind him saw a threatening parabola of fieldsmen waiting for the false shot.

They also shared a common attitude towards bowling: they preferred batting. Lindwall's bias towards it and belief in his own ability in this respect was no less than Miller's. In fact, Lindwall was no mean batsman. If *Wisden*'s definition of 1,500 runs and 75 wickets be taken as the yardstick for determining all-round merit, then Lindwall is eminently qualified, and he played some characteristically robust innings, particularly when Australia were in trouble.

There were differences, of course, both technical and temperamental. Lindwall always had the choice of ends and he invariably bowled with the wind behind him. Before delivering a ball he would go through a routine of touching his toes, swinging his arms, exercising his various muscles, and he progressively increased his pace. Miller, who was always capable of varying his normal twelve-yard run, was at full speed right from the first ball.

Off the field Lindwall was often a very anonymous figure. Nowhere is the fast bowler more venerated than in the West Indies. In 1955 large crowds had gathered to catch their first glimpse of Lindwall. As he alighted from the plane, crowds could hardly believe that this squat figure was the giant bowler about whom they had fantasised. It was only after they had seen him with the ball that they were reassured.

These differences in personality were illustrated by the use they made of their talents. Lindwall, as the name 'killer' – so often applied to him by enthusiastic sub-editors – suggests, was thorough: he destroyed innings. In only three series did he fail to take five or more wickets in an innings and just under half his victims were clean bowled. Miller remained the supreme interventionist. He would remove nos. 1, 2 or 3, or break a major partnership. In only five of his eleven major series did he take five or more wickets in an innings and the great majority of his batsmen were caught or lbw.

Who was the greater bowler? Lindwall, in the opinion of many, had all the virtues: speed, control over swing and swerve, unsettling variations and a vicious bouncer. In run-up approach and acceleration he was considered the nearest approximation to the ideal, though his action was slightly round-arm. As he developed over the years – by 1953 he had compensated for the drop in speed by adding the in-swinger to his repertoire – his action was to produce unpredictable dips and swings. As a bowler Miller did not need to develop: he was a natural. Those who played him in 1945 noticed no change in

1956 and the length of his run-up never influenced his speed; he was just as quick after a four-yard run-up as after a twenty. Yet his action, high and very straight, was pure classicism. It enabled him, in the words of Trevor Bailey, 'to bowl a very good, a very steep bouncer'. Day in and day out Lindwall was probably the greater bowler – Jim Laker's idea of heaven would be Lindwall at one end and Bedi at the other. But Miller trumped him with his unpredictability. Trevor Bailey again: 'Lindwall was superb, but he was known. Miller was always the great unknown, particularly with the old ball.'

Let the last word rest with Jack Fingleton, who has seen most of the prominent fast bowlers of the last thirty years and played against a good many of them. In his brilliant essay, *The Fast Men,* he discusses Larwood, Lindwall and Miller:

> I can see them all again, Larwood gliding in, Lindwall doing his calisthenics as he warms up, Miller clapping his hands and tossing his mane. Those are the three I put on a pedestal, with Larwood of 1932-33, and considering the batting strength against him, possibly just a shade ahead. If I try, I think I can almost hear again the angry thunder of the Hill.

10

For Miller, if an English tour always provided a world stage, it also followed a pattern. The batsman would begin in dazzling form, then fade away into the lesser delights of bowling, while the man, revelling in the spotlight, would play a variety of rôles. For the culture hawk there were the arts of an old continent, for the colonial there were visits to racecourses where by now a Miller bet on a Scobie Breasley horse would inevitably reduce the odds, and for the ladies' man there was an eager audience who followed his every move.

1953 was no exception, though the diversions began early. Miller's ship made its traditional stop at Naples. Miller took Lindwall to see the San Carlos Opera House and was enticed by the music of *La Bohème*. Meanwhile, the doorkeeper who had reluctantly let them watch what was a private rehearsal locked the door and went to fetch the carabinieri. It required nifty work by Lindwall in wrenching the door free and fairly swift running for the pair to avoid the chasing carabinieri and reach the ship seconds before it sailed.

Before the tour began there were other moments of diversion. On arrival at Southampton the Australian manager, George Davies, declared that there would be no bouncers. Hassett hastily retrieved the situation. The day after they arrived, Miller and Lindwall were on TV. Nets were rigged up at Alexandra Palace and the pair provided vicarious thrills by bowling into the camera. Later on in the season, there were to be BBC cameras on the balcony outside the dressing rooms: television had come to stay.

There was one further diversion – which ended in tragedy – before the traditional opening at Worcester. East Molesey, a country club on the Thames, was celebrating its centenary and the Australians reluctantly agreed to play. The match offered a challenge. 140 yards from the pitch, in the middle of the Thames, stood Tagg's Island. Nobody had ever landed a six there and a prize of over six hundred pounds was offered. The newspapers freely speculated about Miller's chances: he failed by ten yards. But the tragedy lay elsewhere. Bill Johnston injured his knee and was never to be fully match-fit on the tour; this was greatly to increase Miller's bowling burden.

The Australians were under severe scrutiny at Worcester. The team was not particularly highly rated and the burden of history seemed to point towards certain conclusions. The parallels with the past, particularly 1926, were overwhelming and for England comforting. The Second World War, like the First, had caused greater dislocation in England, and recovery had been slower. The end of both wars had seen relatively weak English teams soundly beaten and both in 1921 and 1948 Australian touring teams had won with the same weapon: a pair of fast bowlers. Then there had been a solitary victory in the last Test of a lost rubber: Gilligan's in 1924-25, Brown's in 1950-51. So, metaphorically, all English eyes were on the Oval for a repetition of the triumph that brought back the Ashes in 1926. This was Coronation year, Everest was conquered, Churchill was back in power and, probably for the last time, the English world believed that God was still an Englishman.

Miller, conscious that the recent Australian Test record concealed deficiencies and that nine of the players had never played in England before, immediately assumed the rôle of the Godfather. He went out to bat on a cold, blustery Worcester day, with Australia 28 for three in reply to Worcestershire's 333. He was dropped by the wicket-keeper off the first ball, but after that did not make a mistake. In six and a quarter hours he made 220 not out. He added 198 with Hole for the fourth wicket, 116 with Benaud for the sixth, 171 with Archer for the seventh. All of them were playing their first innings in England and he nursed and guided them.

In the next match at Leicester he protected his fellow batsmen from the exiled Sydney spinner, Walsh, and made 42 before being run out. Against Yorkshire, following that, he threatened to annihilate Wardle, but then Craig was run out and he was once again the Miller of 1953. In five and a half hours he made 159 not out and shared in two century stands in a match-winning score of 453. At one stage the Bradford crowd slow-handclapped him but he had not forgotten how to amuse. When after a possible run-out he smacked the provocatively placed bottom of Brennan, the wicket-keeper, the crowd laughed.

By 12 May he had scored 421 runs in three innings, once out, and an English bowler was still to get his wicket. The crowd were seeing a new Miller: patient, responsible, reliable. The Press were convinced that, with a maximum five matches left, the 1,000 runs in May was a distinct possibility. Miller himself seemed to endorse this. He told Fingleton, 'Now, when I see a skipper place a tight field to me and expect me to perform miracles to get runs, I just say, "All right by me, Charlie. I can play that game too".' At that time only six batsmen had achieved the feat, with Don Bradman the only overseas player, though since then another overseas player, Glenn Turner, has joined the select company.

On 13 May the Australians began their match against Cambridge and Miller opened the innings. But Newmarket was only a few miles away and jockey Billy Snaith had given him a reassuring tip. Miller made a quick 20 and was out flashing outside his off-stump. While the other Australians enjoyed themselves Miller backed a succession of losers, so much so that he did not have the money to back the one winning tip that he had been given – Sir Gordon Richards on Pinza – and only just enough to get back. As he arrived he saw the Australians take the field.

In his next three innings till the end of May Miller made 39 runs, with a highest score of 20 against Lancashire. He was not to reach his 1,000 till the return match against Lancashire in the second week of August. Not that Miller showed any concern while losing one of cricket's rare prizes: at Oxford a

week after the Cambridge match, he twitted an under-
graduate who had a complicated run-up, 'Which pitch is he
going to bowl on?' Two balls later Miller was clean bowled
for 19. And his 20 against Lancashire were, says Miller, 'the
happiest runs of my life'. As he waited, padded up, the
Goodwood Stewards Cup was run. Miller had backed a horse
called Matador and just as he was about to walk out Matador
won.

At this stage of the tour – the end of May – the Australians
had won six of their nine matches, all by an innings. The
newcomers were shaping up well and Harvey was
in devastating form. It was difficult for Miller to keep up his
father figure rôle. Already he had bowled 110 overs and there
had been his traditional success at Lord's: while Queen Salote
of Tonga watched and preparations went on for the
Coronation, Miller, his sense of occasion acute, removed the
MCC openers, Simpson and Sheppard, within fifteen runs and
finished with four for 47. He also considerably surprised Tom
Graveney, who was yet to become familiar with his ways, by
bowling him a fast googly for his first ball. (Miller was one of
the few cricketers who could bowl such a ball.)

The stage seemed set for the bowler. But on 4 June, playing
against Sussex, he injured his rib muscles and this seemed to
cast a shadow over his bowling prospects for the entire tour.
There was speculation that he might not bowl again on the
tour and in the First Test he was played as a batsman.

The First Test was Bedser's match. He took fourteen for 99
and rain, arguably, saved the Australians. Miller figured in
the only confident Australian batting of the match. On the
first day, coming in with Australia 128 for 3 – all three wickets
to Bedser – he stayed to make 55 and put on 109 with Hassett,
who made the first of his two centuries in the series.

This partnership had only contained Bedser, not conquered
him. In the second innings Bedser routed the Australians.
After Miller had made 5 he was presented with a Bedser full
toss. In the second innings of the MCC match Miller had taken
a wicket with a full toss and another with a round-arm. When
Bedser had teased him he had responded with, 'Oh Alec, you

want to try slinging up some muck now and then. It comes off
sometimes'.

At Trent Bridge in the First Test, as Miller hit the full toss
straight to Kenyon and walked away, Bedser was ready.
'Thanks for the tip at Lord's,' he said.

The Australian batting continued to crumble, and some
time before Tallon, the no. 8 came out to bat, there were
discussions about appealing against the light. Although
Tallon had not taken part in the discussions, Hassett
instructed him as he walked out, 'All right, Don, give it a go.'
When Tallon swung at his first ball Hassett was not
particularly worried; it seemed a good ruse before an appeal
to the umpires. It was only when Tallon repeated the same
stroke for the third successive time that Hassett, to his dismay,
understood. Tallon had interpreted the instructions as calling
for a furious assault on the bowling. Before Hassett could
intervene, Tallon went on to become the second highest
scorer and Australia were all out for 123.

But rain or no rain and however bad the cricket, Miller
continued to enjoy life. After the First Test the Australians
moved north. While Hassett, George Davies and Morris went
back to London, Miller was left in charge of the team to play
Yorkshire at Sheffield. The match started on a Saturday. That
evening Miller organised a party: 'Right, boys, enjoy
yourselves.' Leadbeater, who had been hired by the manager
to assist him, used his amateur theatrical experience to recite
monologues and limericks, the night was cold, a log fire was
lit and Gil Langley was so carried away by the spirit of the
party that he fell into the fire and had to be dragged away, feet
first, with his jacket still smouldering. It was some time on
Sunday that the party finally ran out of steam.

Monday morning, as Basil Easterbrook recalls, was lovely
and bright. He was on the point of leaving for the match when
the manageress informed him that both Mr Miller and Mr
Lindwall were still in their rooms. Easterbrook hurried there.
Miller and Lindwall were throwing clothes on, the alarm had
not rung, the rest of the team were already on their way to the
match, there wasn't a great deal of time left. Grindleford,

where the Australians were staying, is a picturesque, Swiss resort-type village overlooking a valley; there was no question of taxis. In 1953 a Yorkshire match was almost like a Sixth Test. Bramall Lane would be packed. With the Australians fielding, Miller would be expected to lead the side out and nobody had yet kept Bramall Lane waiting. Then Easterbrook recalled that a local funeral parlour had a black limousine. The funeral parlour was willing and the limousine was procured. By the time it arrived at the ground there were only a few minutes before start of play and the 30,000 crowd were expectantly looking at their watches. Miller jumped out of the limousine and, still getting his clothes together, shouted to Easterbrook, 'Pay the cab, Bas, and collect it from Davies.' He rushed inside the pavilion and changed just in time to lead the Australians out.

The fare came to £2 but George Davies refused to entertain the claim. He suggested that Easterbrook write to the Australian Board of Control. Though £2 was a fair bit of money in 1953, Easterbrook reluctantly decided to forget about the whole thing. Almost twenty years later, the 1972 Australians were playing at Old Trafford. There was rain and, as is Easterbrook's habit, he was quietly reading a book. Lindwall came up to him and thrust £5 into his pocket. 'That's for Grindleford, Bas.'

Easterbrook, whose concern for the correct literary phrase is as great as his concern for correctness in financial matters, reminded him that it was £2.

Lindwall said, 'Well, Bas, there's been inflation and it's been a long time.'

Now, in June 1953, the figure of Bailey interposed. The war with the Roundheads was resumed. Miller began well: in the first innings of the Lord's Test he secured his first wicket of the series, Bailey caught and bowled. So great was his delight that he threw the ball up a number of times and surprised Bailey with his immoderate glee. Then came his most significant innings of the series, Australia's highest total and her best chance of victory. This was Miller the responsible. Australia were 3 for 1 in the second innings when he arrived, 235 for 4 when he left, a useful lead of 209 with England batting last. There was not a single six in his 109 but there were two significant partnerships: 165 with Morris, 59 with Harvey. It was not slow – 111 runs were added in two hours at one stage – there were just no flamboyant flourishes.

But if the going was often grim on the field, off it there was time for some characteristic Miller humour. As tradition required, both teams were presented to the Queen during the Test. Players of both teams knew how historic the occasion was, but with about five minutes left the Australians discovered that they were without Keith Miller. Just as the teams were about to line up, he arrived with beads of perspiration glistening on his forehead. 'Where have you been?' asked his team-mates. Miller replied, 'I don't know. Where am I now?'

The worth of his innings was underlined by the subsequent Australian batting. Soon after he was out there was a collapse, and only a powerfully hit Lindwall 50, with two sixes and five fours enabled Australia to finish with 368.

That evening the Australians sensed a win – England, requiring 343 to win, were 21 for 3 with Hutton, Kenyon and Graveney out – and celebrated. They watched *Guys and Dolls* at the Coliseum, attended a back-stage party and went on to the Café de Paris. Gloom settled over English cricket. John Arlott wrote in his diary, 'There is no sign of rain.' Next morning *The Daily Telegraph* observed, 'Late last night there was no queue outside Lord's'.

It was to be an agonisingly long six hours: Compton lasted one and a half, Bailey, chewing hard on his gum, occupied four, Watson almost six, including half-an-hour the previous evening. At five minutes to three, with Lord's filling up, Hassett took the new ball and brought on Miller and Lindwall. English cricket held its breath. Five overs, five runs; drinks, five overs, four runs, no wicket; they did not bowl again as a pair. England were safe. It marked the first significant defeat for Lindwall and Miller, yet a defeat that spoke eloquently of their psychological hold on English cricket. This was the fifth day's play, the wicket was taking spin, Australia had three spinners; if anybody could have won the match for Australia it should have been their spinners. Yet even at six o'clock when Bailey and Watson were out in quick succession and Brown and Evans were together, there were anxious looks every time Hassett passed Lindwall or Miller. Both Brown and Evans were susceptible to pace and a few overs of quick bowling, it was felt, might have secured an Australian victory. But Hassett did not call on the pair, the moment passed and English cricket began to believe in itself: Lindwall and Miller could be contained.

The Australians, frustrated and bewildered, looked for an explanation beyond the game to the social activities of their cricketers. The Australian Press had already carried critical stories and the entertainments of the penultimate day drew the greatest fire. Finally, Davies had to issue an explanatory statement. He was personally satisfied that every member of the team was in bed by 1 a.m. on that crucial Tuesday morning.

For Miller the fun appeared to have gone out of the game. In the Third Test at Old Trafford only thirteen hours' play was possible. The wicket was a typical and treacherous English 'turner' and he bowled off-spinners mostly round the wicket. The festival cricket at the Hague, when he dazzled the Dutchmen with his footwork, revived his interest, and with the Queen and the Duke of Edinburgh present at the Middlesex–Australia match at Lord's, he turned on the batting fireworks. He made 71, his highest score in the county matches since the second week of May – this was the third week of July – and hit another of those straight, spectacular sixes. It seemed a happy prelude to the Fourth Test at Leeds.

There had been rain at Leeds, water had seeped under the covers, the wicket was greasy and Hassett asked England to bat. There was speculation that his motives were more respect for English bowlers on a drying wicket than hope of quick success. Now, in such unfavourable conditions, Lindwall and Miller responded with their best bowling of the tour as a pair. Lindwall bowled Hutton with the second ball of the match and took the wickets of Compton, Watson,

Simpson and Evans: five for 54; Miller had Edrich and Graveney: two for 39. England made 167.

In the second innings, after England through Compton and Edrich had whittled away Australia's lead of 99, Lindwall and Miller produced their second great spell of the match in the most unfavourable circumstances – fourth and fifth day wickets. Lindwall started it with the new ball, Miller continued with the slightly worn. Lindwall removed Edrich; Miller, in successive deliveries, removed Watson and Simpson. Then he injured Compton and early on the fifth day removed Evans. England had been reduced to 182 for 6 – 83 ahead – not much after 12 o'clock on the last day. But there was Bailey.

The previous evening Bailey had prevented a Miller hat trick. Now he began to deny him with that most characteristic shot of his, the forward defensive prod. Alan Ross once described Bailey's Test repertoire as being 'limited to three strokes: the forward defensive, the late cut and the swing to leg with the ratio in favour of the first about one hundred to one'. On this day Miller must have felt the ratio to be nearer a thousand to one, so unfailingly did Bailey provide the same answer to whatever he presented.

Then two minutes before lunch, under a cloudless blue sky, Bailey appealed against the light. The Australians, who had taken to referring to him as 'Sir Laurence' (after Olivier) did not even wait for the decision. Miller, still amused, it would appear, gathered up the bails at his end and presented them to the umpires as they were holding their conference. That was to be the last bit of humour for the day.

Bailey continued his resistance. Umpire Chester, with what the Australians thought was unnecessary histrionics, turned down several appeals. (Hassett was later to ask that Chester should not be considered for the Oval; after being named he withdrew because, it was said, of illness.) Then, towards the end of Bailey's vigil of four hours and twenty minutes, with England reasonably secure, came the moment the day had been leading up to.

Bailey, who in 215 balls made seventeen scoring strokes,

suddenly hit a four, one of only two in his innings. Miller reacted with a beamer to which Bailey ducked. Next ball he appealed unsuccessfully for lbw. Then, just as he was about to begin his run, Bailey held up a hand, calmly moved aside and fastidiously adjusted his glove. Fingleton thought Miller would explode. But he walked across to Lindwall fielding at cover, they sat down for a chat, and he only resumed bowling when he was certain Bailey was prepared.

But the crowd had already adopted Bailey (this was the day, it was said, that Bailey was naturalised as a Yorkshireman) and as Miller returned to the pavilion at the end of the English innings a spectator shouted, 'You bloody great Australian prawn.'

Miller grabbed him, saying, 'Here you, come with me, I've got something to say to you,' and hustled him to the pavilion and a waiting policeman.

At first the man, 'elderly, soberly dressed', protested innocence: 'It was the man next to me who shouted.' But, confronted by the repercussions of a possible court case, he soon changed his tune.

This drained Miller's anger and in much better humour, while admitting that Bailey had 'irritated' him, he explained to the Press that he had got hold of the wrong man. It remains one of the few moments in his career when he lost his ability to control a crowd. Even earlier in the same day he had converted crowd anger to humour, and the later incident provides an indication of how completely Bailey succeeded in riling him.

Miller did not bat in the Australian second innings when Bailey came on with leg-theory bowling and prevented what looked like an irresistible Australian chase for victory. At the end of the match Bailey had to be spirited away to escape adoring crowds.

Miller's frustration continued into the Oval Test. He bowled forty-five overs for two wickets in the match and made 1 in the first innings (lbw Bailey – see plate 10) and 0 in the second (c Trueman b Laker) when sixteen deliveries by Laker and Lock saw four wickets fall for 2 runs and settled the match, the series and the Ashes. Since his Lord's century Miller's Test scores had been 17, 6, 5, 1, 0 and his bowling read: 144 overs, 58 maidens, 229 runs and 9 wickets.

The Roundheads' triumph was complete. Bailey, by completely blunting Australia's principal match-winner at Lord's and Leeds, had made the Oval possible. By the end of the series Bailey was being seriously promoted as the leading all-rounder in the world.

And that, for the purpose of our story is highly inconvenient. The wrong man had won. Natural justice, an innate sense of beauty, the instinctive partiality towards skill, the desire for fantasy, love for brave and handsome causes – all pointed towards Miller. Bailey should not have lived on the same field with him. Even the most partisan of Bailey's fans – and he always evoked extremely partisan loyalties – would concede that Miller was in a different, superior class. Bailey himself cheerfully admits to his technical limitations, but cricket arguments have never been resolved solely on the basis of technical eloquence. In Bailey, Miller had met one of the keenest and shrewdest students of the game of cricket has produced, one who had studied his rival well. Miller was excitable: nag him and he will rise to the bait; bowl persistently on his leg-stump and he will have a swing; indulge in calculated mannerisms and there may be a self-destroying reaction.

To the English, Miller personified the Australian approach to the game and Australia always brought out the best, or the worst, in Bailey. Umpire Dai Davies describes a typical scene:

> They always let him have one ball first. Trevor would duck and come up again chewing, and then a very superior smile would come over his face. He had them beaten at the nerve-war in the middle and he knew it.

Today it is hard to imagine watching this comfortable, middle-aged man who gives his opinions with such care and precision (rare in a cricketer turned writer) that in those days he aroused such deep and bitter feelings among the Australians. Then, even Jack Fingleton was moved to write after the Leeds incident, 'I began to think that Bailey had forgotten where he was and imagined himself at Lord's in the annual Oxford–Cambridge game, a post-war game in which, I am told, no holds are barred.' Among Australians the feelings persisted that Bailey (Dulwich College and Cambridge) was demonstrating to the colonial the virtue of superior ways.

There was another factor. Bailey did not move in Miller's social circle. Though they played in four series, never did Bailey visit the Miller home. It was not an exclusive circle, but temperamentally Bailey did not belong. In fact, he did not socialise a great deal with his contemporaries, so the humour that tempered a Miller–Compton duel was absent.

However, the Miller–Bailey duels should not obscure the overall friendliness of the series, nor did they affect Miller's position as a substantial public figure: he was always news. The day after the Oval Test the *Star* reported:

> One of the first things Australian all-rounder Keith Miller did after the fate of the Ashes had been decided was to make a phone call to America. But his American wife, Peggy, on holiday in Boston with the three Miller boys aged 5, 3 and 2, knows nothing about cricket and had little idea of what had been going on at the Oval. The boys, however, were glad to ask for some details.

After the Oval there was no Bailey, and Miller's batting immediately prospered. He made 67 against the Gentlemen, 68 against Kent and then did what all Australia had been longing to do: put that upstart Trueman in his place.

Trueman had been held up as the avenging English hero of the historical wounds inflicted by Lindwall and Miller. English sailors had shouted his name as the Australians sailed for England, the English Press had invoked his deeds, English crowds had warned of his coming. Yet Trueman proved elusive and did not bowl his first over against the Australians until 15 August in the Fifth Test. It was an inconclusive affair: Trueman was useful, the Australians preoccupied with tackling the spin of Laker and Lock. Then came the match against the Combined Services. Trueman opened the bowling, Miller came in to bat with Australia 2 for 1. In 238 minutes he made 200. He finished with 262 not out and with de Courcy he put on 377 in 205 minutes. Trueman's first six overs cost 36 runs – 12 in one over to Miller – and he finished with 14 – 2 – 95 – 0. Miller's joy was complete. As he came in he handed his bat to a schoolboy.

The tour also appeared to have resolved one old question. Miller was now being considered solely as a batsman. Though his batting record for the Tests was poor – 223 runs for an average of 24.78 – he was second in the tour averages with 1,433 runs for an average of 51.18. And his bowling underlined the supposed gap: ten wickets at a cost of 30 runs each in the Tests; forty-five wickets at a cost of 22.51 runs each on the tour. He was the least effective of the major Australian bowlers. Fingleton suggested that 'he must now be allowed to die a very honourable death as a bowler'. Yet within fifteen months he was to produce some of the fastest and best bowling of his career.

11

Though this was not immediately apparent, Miller had entered a new and final phase of his career. He was now a member of losing Australian sides. His efforts would continue to be spectacular and often significant, but they were no longer to be that decisive. They created a poignancy which had never before been associated with his play, a poignancy heightened by the answer provided to the central question of the period: would Miller captain Australia?

A Miller captaincy had been persistent post-Bradman rumour; Robertson-Glasgow was writing about it as early as December 1949. But in the winter of 1953-54 it could no longer be avoided. Hassett had retired at the end of the previous English tour, the team had to be rebuilt and Australian cricket had to recapture the crowds which it had lost, largely to tennis and a more emphatic outdoor way of life.

Miller was quick to advertise his claims. He led New South Wales to their first Sheffield Shield under his captaincy, with only one loss in seven matches. He headed the batting with 510 runs for an average of 63.75 though his bowling was slightly expensive: fourteen wickets at a cost of 28 runs each. Outside the Shield he made a century in each innings of the Hassett Testimonial Match. So, as the 1954-55 season opened he was established as the public favourite, ahead of his only possible rivals: Arthur Morris and Ian Johnson.

Morris, a dapper, neat batsman, had never really recaptured his early post-war dominance and had had rather the worst of his historic duels with Bedser. But he was still a considerable influence in Australian cricket and almost universally liked. His tactical ability was never questioned, and he had been a successful vice-captain on tours though he had a reputation for being 'soft': it was said that he was likely to allow emotional considerations to influence his decisions. His cricket relationship with Miller was awkward. At the State level he played under Miller, at the national level the positions were reversed, but this never affected their personal friendship.

Ian Johnson, on a strict examination of cricket ability, appeared the least likely choice. Of the three, his position in the team was the most doubtful. He had not been selected to tour England in 1953 and as captain of Victoria he had not revealed either startling originality or inventive brilliance. But the choice of a cricket captain, particularly at the international level, has never been governed by purely technical arguments, and in the wider sense Johnson stood supreme. Son of a former Australian selector, married to the daughter of another, he had the right background. He was educated at Wesley College which boasted distinguished alumni including the then prime minister, Robert Menzies. He had the necessary diplomatic reputation – it was said he could smile in seven different ways at the same time and not mean any one of them, but that in a diplomat is a virtue, not a weakness. He could be expected to say the right thing at the right time with the proper intonation, and he had the appropriate power-base, Victoria, still the final arbiter Australian cricket.

The final decision rested with the Australian Board of Control. It was not known for any bias towards Miller and that summer New South Wales were not the best of sponsors: the echoes of the Sid Barnes libel case, when three New South Wales Board members had in effect testified against the Board, were still being felt. Also, the Board's preferences were known: for the 1953 English tour Miller had been replaced by Morris after only one season as vice-captain.

But as Hutton's team arrived in Australia, Miller continued to be the public favourite. He played two matches before the team for the First Test was announced. New South Wales won the Shield match against Queensland on first innings and in the MCC match only a Cowdrey century in each innings prevented a victory.

Two days later the Australian team was announced and Ian Johnson was named captain. Whitington guesstimated that Victoria and South Australia voted for Johnson, New South Wales for Miller and Queensland for Morris. The *Sydney Daily Telegraph* in an editorial spoke about 'strong feeling among cricket enthusiasts that "horse trading" on a State basis rather than objective evaluation of cricket skill has dominated selectors' discussions'. The controversy provoked by the decision never abated and was to continue right through the season.

If Miller was angry he did not show it. He wanted to captain Australia and made no secret of his belief that New South Wales under him were superior to Johnson's Australia. He proved this amply when his New South Wales played MCC. In mid-February after the Fourth Test had conclusively decided the series in England's favour, MCC returned to Sydney. Owing to the effects of vaccination (with a West Indies tour coming), New South Wales were without Morris and Watson. But two of Miller's youngsters – Philpott and Booth, selected at the last minute – made significant runs in the first innings. Miller himself made 71 in the second and on the last day broke the potentially match-winning stand between May and Hutton by bowling May. New South Wales won by 45 runs. It was only the second defeat MCC suffered on tour and the only one outside the Tests.

Miller completed his reply to the selectors in the domestic matches. Despite his absence from two of the four matches owing to Test calls, his protégés – Davidson, Burke, Simpson, Crawford and Benaud – had done enough for New South Wales to emerge as winners of the Sheffield Shield for the second successive time. By then Australian cricket was in a state of considerable chaos.

The story of the 1954-55 Tests is part of the folklore of modern English cricket. Hutton arrived with five possible opening bowlers, four of whom played in the first Test.

Hutton won the toss and on a wicket advertised as a 'demon wicket' ideal for pace asked Australia to bat. The wicket turned out to be placid and the four England quick bowlers – Bedser, Statham, Bailey and Tyson – conceded a hundred runs each. Australia made 601 and won the match by an innings. In the next match at Sydney Hutton dropped Bedser and on the first day England were all out for 154 (Wardle with 35 was the top scorer). But then in the heat and on a fifth-day wicket Statham and Tyson by sheer pace bowled England to victory: a new fast bowling pair had emerged. In the next two Tests they took twenty-five wickets between them and for the first time since the war English pace won the final argument.

Undoubtedly the series will be remembered for Tyson's historic performances, yet Miller produced two spells of fast bowling as memorable as any in the series. He had begun with the usual statements: he wanted to concentrate on batting, his bowling was to be incidental. There was also this season a new complication: his knee had begun to trouble him. In the first Test he made 49 in eighty-five minutes, an innings which charmed all the observers. His bowling was arithmetically slight – two for 49 in twenty-three overs – but the arithmetic concealed the hostility and intent of his opening spell when Lindwall and he reduced the English first innings to 11 for 3, Miller taking one wicket, Lindwall two. But with the suspect knee now joining the well advertised back, fast bowling interventions by Miller were considered unlikely and the English batsmen were reassured.

They were delighted when they heard two days before the Second Test that a knee injury would keep Miller out of the Test. Though Hutton with mock grief told the Press that he was sorry his old friend, Mr Miller, was unable to play, he was genuinely relieved and regaled pressmen with one of the few jokes of their great post-war duels. 'In 1945', recalled Hutton, 'Miller had dinner with my wife and myself, and he told me he thought I had a very nice wife. When I came out here in 1946 Miller was bowling and after he had sent me four or five bouncers I wondered whether he had forgotten our dinner. So when I got to his end I said, "My wife sends you her love". But that did not make any difference. Keith still bowled bumpers at me'.

England easily won the Second Test to level the series but even as the teams assembled for the Third at Melbourne it appeared extremely doubtful whether Miller would bowl. He had had virtually no competitive cricket for a month, and the day before the match the doctor advised caution. On the morning of the match Miller tried out his knee in his hotel bedroom and just before play started he told Johnson he would like to test it, perhaps for a couple of overs.

Melbourne on New Year's Eve provided a grassy wicket – lifeless brown rather than green – and sticky heat. Australia lost the toss – always, Miller maintained, a vital factor at Melbourne. Lindwall bowled the first over, then Miller produced what Arlott called 'one of the most vivid opening spells I have ever seen'. Within quarter of an hour he forced Edrich into a leg-glance and Lindwall took the catch: 14 for 1. Seven runs later Miller beat Hutton with sheer pace and Hole at first slip took the catch: 21 for 2. At ten minutes to one he got one to lift and Compton, back after two Tests, was caught off his glove by Harvey: 29 for 3. Miller's three wickets cost five runs. At lunch England were 59 for 4 and the advantage of the toss was an inconvenient memory. Miller's analysis read 9 – 8 – 5 – 3. There had been only two scoring strokes off him, cover-drives for three and two by Compton and Cowdrey.

But Johnson could not – would not – risk Miller's knee any further. He bowled two more overs in the innings, Cowdrey made a century, May made 91 in the second innings and Miller took only one more wicket in the match, that of Evans late in the second innings. Then came Tyson's historic spell to decide the match. Australia were left 240 to win and began the last day requiring 165 with eight wickets in hand. With the seventh ball of the day Tyson removed Harvey. Miller came in and, on a wicket supposedly made for spinners, Australia's main enemy appeared to be Appleyard.

As Miller settled down at the crease Gubby Allen turned to Sir Robert Menzies, sitting next to him, and said: 'I don't think your friend is going to make any runs today'.

Sir Robert Menzies raised his eyebrows, 'Why?' – an indication of displeasure rather than enquiry.

Tyson's first ball beat Miller completely. In the next over Miller faced four shooters from Statham. He stopped three and from the fourth scored a boundary between his pads and his leg stump. Two runs later Tyson got one to lift and Edrich did the rest. As Miller walked back to the pavilion, Sir Robert Menzies turned to Gubby Allen and said, 'I've learned something today'.

Tyson took two further wickets to finish with seven for 27. Statham took two for 38 and seventy-nine minutes after play had started England won the match.

Three weeks later the teams went to Adelaide for the crucial Fourth Test. For four days the match proceeded conventionally. Australia made 323, Miller making 44; England replied with 341 and at the end of the fourth day's play Australia were 69 for 3. Then in ninety minutes of the fifth morning Tyson and Statham took six wickets between them and soon after lunch England required 94 to retain the Ashes. No task could have appeared simpler. The Australians were completely demoralised. The wicket, despite the achievements of Tyson and Statham, appeared to be slow and there was very nearly a day and a half in which to make the runs. Also, there was no Lindwall, who had injured his leg in a State match.

The situation had just the right appeal for Miller. In his first over Miller bowled Edrich with the first ball he faced. In his second over he had Hutton caught by Davidson. In his third he had Cowdrey caught by Archer. Miller had bowled twenty balls, England were 18 for 3. The England dressing room was in a state of chaos. Hutton, convinced that his great dream was over, could not bear to watch the play and kept pacing up and down, muttering, 'That old so-and-so has done us in again'. As if in acknowledgement, three RAAF Meteor jets swooped down on the Adelaide ground and dipped their wings. Just as they did so Miller nearly caught and bowled May.

But Johnson rested Miller and as soon as he was taken off the game changed character: the batsmen began to look secure.

Again Miller intervened. May had begun to middle his drives, but he could not quite keep one down and Miller acrobatically took the catch: 49 for 4. Miller could do no more. Bailey and Compton held firm and though Bailey was out to Johnston, Compton and Evans saw matters through with Evans winning a little argument. Compton would have won £5 if he had repeated his Ashes-winning hit of the Oval, but Evans kept the strike, made the winning hit and Compton comforted himself with swear-words.

So, in the early months of 1955, with a visit to the West Indies impending, Australian cricket found itself bewildered, helpless, and once again in search of a leader. It was not so much the margin of defeat that hurt, though that was bad enough – three Test matches to one, the worst since Jardine's visit in 1932–33 – but the psychological overtones. The Australians had been beaten by weapons that they had long considered their exclusive preserve: a pair of fast bowlers producing total, complete destruction. Deficiencies which had never been suspected were now magnified. The Australians played cross-bat shots, they cut perilously close to the stumps, they swished outside the off-stump. The apocryphal witticism of the barracker of Sydney Hill summed up the national mood. As a particular batsman played and missed at Tyson time after time, the Hillite cried out, 'Bowl 'im a grand piano and see if he can play it'.

Again, Miller was offered as captain. If nothing else he might rectify this collective failure of nerve. Again the selectors preferred Ian Johnson. But there was, perhaps, some logic, though largely non-cricketing, for this apparent madness. The MCC tour of the West Indies the previous winter had been a remarkable story of bitterness and animosity. There had been a riot in one Test and in two others umpires and their relations were threatened with physical violence. Nothing like it had ever been seen on a cricket field, Jardine's tour of Australia not excepted.

What really frightened the cricket administrators was that the causes were not directly related to cricket. Today when no cricket administrator should consider his education complete unless he has a working knowledge of the South African Parliament and barbed wire surrounding cricket pitches is not an unheard-of phenomenon, the incidents and the reaction may appear exaggerated. But in the fifties with the cricket world still believing that the game was divinely protected from mundane considerations, the tour came as a great shock. The politics of racial and social change were fast catching up with cricket – it was another seventeen years before its full impact was felt – and apart from pious resolutions and a sense of hurt and confused anger the cricket world had little to offer.

It was against this backdrop that the Australians undertook their first tour of the West Indies. Their administrators, keen to forestall the slightest provocation, and looking for a captain for a white team from a country with certain pronounced racial policies, settled for dependable dullness rather than unpredictable brilliance. Johnson might not be inspiring but he would always know the right phrases. Diplomacy was preferred to cricket.

The Australians were never to be completely immune from the wider implications during their 1955 tour. In three Tests the West Indies were captained by Dennis Atkinson. Atkinson was white, he was a Barbadian, he had been preferred to Worrell: there were demonstrations. And West Indies team selections, which were a fragile balance of inter-island loyalties, talents and prejudices, caused confusion and bitterness. But compared to the MCC visit this was a blissfully happy tour apart from the usual reactions to the bumpers of Lindwall and Miller.

Miller the man was instantly popular and almost universally respected. As soon as the Australians arrived in Jamaica he noticed a diffident Valentine standing outside the main airport reception hall and brought him in from the heat. He marched to the office of Lawrence Roberts, Sports Editor of the *Daily Gleaner*, and announced, 'I'm Miller. What's your name and what do you want to know?' And he held his own in the different and often conflicting strata of society. He kept a Governor waiting and arrived just in time for a Test Match. In

Jamaica he ran off the field and sipped Coca Cola with the crowd. In Barbados he successfully and hilariously imitated the seductive habit of the women of carrying heavy items on their heads. And inevitably there was a Miller contribution to the carefree West Indian life. In Antigua a girl had introduced herself to Keith and said, 'I've got a photograph of you at the end of my bed.'

Gil Langley overheard this conversation and as the party flew out of Antigua he jokingly asked Keith, 'Did you ever get to see the photograph?'

Keith smiled. 'Yes, but it's not at the end of the bed'.

As a cricketer he was to enjoy his best international series. The First Test set the pattern: he made 147, his highest Test score, and took five wickets; Lindwall took six wickets and Australia won the match by nine wickets with a day to spare. But the real significance of the match lies in the way that Miller, who was tour vice-captain, captained Australia for the first and only time after Johnson had hurt his foot while batting on the second day. He indicated in unmistakable terms that what was good for the Sheffield Shield was good for international cricket. At every twist and turn in the game he took decisions which were often bold, sometimes contro-versial and always decisive.

Now on paper this looks an easy Test match. Australia, having made 515 in the first innings, were always in command. Yet when the West Indies began their reply – which was the moment Miller took over the captaincy – an Australian victory was by no means certain. The West Indies had a formidable batting order: Holt, Weekes, Walcott, Worrell, Collie Smith and Atkinson, all of whom were capable of scoring a century. This was still a good batting wicket and the Australians were without their best spinner, Johnson; the match still had to be won.

On the fourth day Clyde Walcott and Collie Smith resumed the West Indies first innings, fighting to avoid a follow-on. They had already put on 120 and Miller, who had not taken the new ball the previous evening, did not take it first thing in the morning. He took it just when the batsmen

looked like settling in again. Then for the addition of 29 runs
five wickets fell, Miller taking the wickets of Walcott and
Atkinson, Lindwall the wickets of Collie Smith, King and
Valentine.

Now Miller was faced with a decision about enforcing the
follow-on. The wicket was taking spin and a strong West
Indies reply could mean batting on an uncomfortable last-day
wicket. There was also the memory of recent reactions to the
follow-on. Jeff Stollmeyer had not enforced one against
England and only a subsequent England collapse had
prevented a violent crowd reaction. He decided to enforce
the follow-on.

At tea on the fourth day the West Indies were 114 for 1 and
his decision was being widely and critically questioned. Then
Holt who had been the bulwark fell to Benaud and Miller
psyched out Weekes. Miller's bowlers were tired but with
Weekes hesitant he set an intimidating field. Weekes,
desperately trying to add to his 1, fell for the bait. He was
caught and bowled by Benaud.

There remained one other decisive Miller moment. On the
fifth day Walcott and Smith again held up the Australians.
This time he hurried the introduction of the new ball –
thinking it would deviate more – and in three overs Lindwall
and Miller took three wickets for 4 runs. Miller took the
wickets of Smith and Binns, Lindwall that of Walcott. Then
Archer completed the formalities of victory.

In the next two Tests Miller did little. In the drawn Second,
coming in to bat no. 6 after Australia had already made over
300, he made three uninterested runs. He left the bowling to
Lindwall, who took six wickets. In the victorious Third
he thrice removed openers cheaply – Holt (twice) and
Stollmeyer – and made 33 runs.

It was Barbados and Everton Weekes that revived him.
Weekes that season was completely overshadowed by
Walcott. The three W's had their own distinct periods of
dominance and Walcott was in the middle of his. Though
Weekes had begun the series badly he was just coming back to
form and there was still a score to settle with Lindwall and

Miller. Three years ago they had curbed the greatest hooker in the world with a succession of bumpers. On this day, and in front of his home crowd, Weekes was to produce one of the most memorable innings of the tour. While Miller removed Hunte for 0, Collie Smith for 4 and Sobers for 0, Weekes made 100 out of 132, and every time Miller bowled a bouncer Weekes was ready with a murderous hook. In the end, and with the second new ball, Miller did get his revenge. There was yet another bouncer, Weekes hooked, but he was late and was caught: an equality of sorts had been established. Miller took four for 51, Weekes made 132, Barbados made 305. Miller the batsman responded in quality, though not in quantity: he made 36 in thirty-nine minutes before lunging forward and getting out leg-before. The two main participants having played their parts, the lesser lights took over and Australia won their narrowest victory of the series.

The Fourth Test was, in many ways, the most characteristic Miller match of the series. He made a century and he took three wickets, all major West Indian batsmen: Weekes, Smith and Worrell. He amused the crowd, he angered them, he very nearly missed playing in the match.

Twenty minutes before the start there was no sign of him. The teams had already been presented to the Governor, Sir Robert Arundel, but the Australians were yet to decide on their final eleven. Before the match it had been decided that Davidson, the all-rounder, would replace Favell, the opening batsmen, as the twelfth man. On the morning of the match Morris reported unfit and Favell, who had so far been the perennial twelfth man, was called back into the squad. But with Miller's whereabouts a complete mystery the Australians could come to no decision: if he did not turn up, Davidson would have to play to keep the bowling up to strength. Then just as it seemed that the toss could not be delayed – and Johnson would have to reveal his team before that – Miller arrived. His explanation was simple: his driver had got stuck in the Georgetown traffic. Favell was told, 'Get dressed, you're in. And what's more, you open.' Australia won the toss, Favell made 72 and it was evening before Miller had to exert himself.

Just before he went in to bat, Maurice Visbord, a faithful follower of Australian cricket, offered 6 to 4 that Miller would not remain beyond half an hour. The previous evening Miller had philosophised, 'I'm getting too old for late Saturday nights and long Sunday recoveries: and anyhow, you never know, I may be in the field all day tomorrow'. The bet was Visbord's response. But Miller declined to accept. It proved to be a singular error of judgement. Starting his innings in a mini-crisis – Australia had declined from 226 for 2 to 233 for 5 – he batted for 242 minutes making 137, with twenty-two fours. Then with Australia well on their way to 500, he gave himself out. He 'cut' a ball from outside the off-stump, the wicket-keeper 'caught it', he turned and walked towards the pavilion in astonished, absolute silence: nobody had appealed. As he went past the slips Weekes pointed out that the umpire had not given him out. Miller glanced back to see the umpire, Lee Kow, removing the bails for tea. That evening Lee Kow confirmed the story: 'I don't think you hit it and I would have given you the benefit of the doubt'. But Miller was convinced he was out and that was what mattered.

His 'walk' was to have a strange sequel. In the second innings he played forward to Atkinson and was hit on the pads. There was a half appeal, the type bowlers make to indicate moral ascendancy rather than actual success, and Lee Kow gave him out. Later, at a party Lee Kow asked him whether he had played the ball. When Miller assured him he had, Lee Kow apologised.

Australia nevertheless finished their first innings with a mammoth 668. It meant the West Indies would probably have to score over 800 in two days to have any chance of winning, and win they had to if the rubber was to be shared. The West Indies gambled and Sobers opened the batting. There followed a most remarkable innings. In three overs he hit Miller for seven fours: three in the first, three in the second, then a peerless shot through the covers in the third. Miller retired from the bowling crease. In the context of the match it was not very significant. Sobers was out for 43 and it was a later partnership between Atkinson and Depeiza that saved the match for the West Indies. But in retrospect it forms a delicious moment. The all-rounder of the future was proclaiming his genius – within six years the title would be indisputably his.

The match itself provided a platform for Miller to practise one of his cherished beliefs: 'There is a crowd out there going to sleep and I must try and wake them up'. His act started as a comedy and ended in the eyes of the Barbadians with a piece of 'calculated villainy'. From the third day the West Indies were grimly avoiding defeat largely through the record-breaking partnership between Atkinson and Depeiza. Throughout this partnership Miller with inimitable gestures reduced the highly partisan Bridgetown crowd to contagious laughter. Then came the 'villainy'.

In the second innings Australia left the West Indies three hours and fifty minutes in which to get 408. Half an hour before the close the West Indians were 193 for 5, content with a draw and not very eager to face the new ball. Nothing could have been more galling to Miller. He gave away eight runs with an overthrow and four byes and took the new ball. Suddenly the game was transformed. The Australian fielders were running to their umbrella fielding positions, Miller and Lindwall were bowling at full pace and the West Indies were struggling. This continued till the last ball of the match and although Miller could not force a result he had succeeded in reviving a match that had gone to sleep. But few Barbadians appreciated his effort and one commentator even called it 'unfair'.

The last Test was statistically Miller's best. He took eight wickets in the match – six for 107 in the first innings where he caused a collapse from 327 for 5 to 364 all out – and he scored 109, one of five Australian century-makers. These collective efforts provided another easy victory.

So at the end of the series it was all glory for Miller and Australia. He had finished second in the Test batting with an average of 73.16; the Lindwall–Miller partnership had taken forty of the ninety West Indies wickets that fell – twenty each. On plumb batting wickets – Miller felt he could bat on the Bridgetown wicket all day with a teaspoon – and against bowlers who were several yards slower than Tyson, the Australians had completely rehabilitated themselves. The margin of victory had been 3-0; in none of the Tests was the side even remotely in danger; in only one innings did they total less than 500; all the major batsmen had made runs – four averaging over 60 – and the spinners had ably supported the fast bowling pair.

Yet in just over a year post-war Australian cricket was to reach its nadir. England, rain, turning wickets and Laker awaited them, and Miller was to suffer extraordinarily harsh treatment.

12

In November 1955 two events occurred in Miller's personal life. Peggy gave birth to an 8 lb 10 ozs son, their fourth child, and Miller turned thirty-six. In English cricket thirty-six is not considered particularly old: Jack Hobbs was still making first-class centuries at the age of forty-nine, and more recently Cowdrey was worth a Test place in his forties. Even in the Australian generation that preceded Miller the mid-thirties were not an irretrievable turning point. Macartney, Bradman and Hassett were in their forties when they made their last tours of England. And for Miller, who always judged his cricket by challenges, there remained one unconquered pinnacle: the captaincy of Australia.

Despite Johnson's success in the West Indies his chances of captaining the tour party to England in 1956 appeared slim. Memories of his captaincy in the disastrous winter of 1954-55 were still uncomfortably fresh and he had last toured England eight years before, having been passed over in 1953. It had been freely speculated during the West Indies tour that if Miller made a success of the vice-captaincy (no doubts were to be expressed on that score) he would be a certainty for the captaincy in England. So throughout the Australian season there was a steady stream of stories promoting Miller's chances. Their main burden was simple: Miller's playboy days – the factor that had constantly undermined his chances – had been forgiven, and since his cricketing qualities were never in dispute there seemed to be no conceivable obstacle. The Press and the public had no doubts and if a referendum had been held that winter Miller would have been elected captain by a wide margin.

He responded with his best and most characteristic Sheffield Shield performances. He never failed as a batsman, bowler or captain. He hit centuries against Queensland and Western Australia and played usefully in the second match against South Australia: 44 and three for 17. But the season was really remarkable for a sensational piece of bowling and for what *Wisden* called 'one of the most memorable gestures to a sporting crowd in Australia'.

New South Wales's second match of the season was against South Australia at Sydney. On the first day New South Wales made 215 for 8 declared, Miller making 3. By the close of play South Australia were 2 for no loss. When play began the next day Miller still had four balls of an over to complete. At the end of it he walked past Alan Davidson at slip and said, 'I'll have just one more over, there's nothing in the pitch for me. Then you can take over.'

Davidson never did get to bowl. In the next over Miller took three wickets and in another 5.3 overs South Australia were all out for 27 – the lowest score in an inter-State match for seventy-two years. Miller's figures read: 7.3 – 3 – 12 – 7. It was the best performance ever recorded in the Shield. As he came into the dressing room a reporter asked him the reasons.

'Ah, well there are three reasons', Miller replied. 'The first one is I bowled bloody well, the second one is . . . er . . . hmm . . . ah . . . Well, you can forget about the other two.'

The gesture came appropriately enough in the drawn match against Victoria. Victoria won the toss and batted. There was persistent rain, but 10,625 Melbourne spectators had braved the weather and Miller refused to ask for an adjournment. It meant that New South Wales had to play with a greasy ball and Victoria recovered from 110 for 5 to 277 all out. The gesture could not have come at a better moment. In practical terms it amounted to little since the match was drawn, but it meant that the Melbourne crowd did see some play and it effectively marked Miller's farewell to Melbourne.

A week later – over the New Year – New South Wales played Queensland. Miller, who had made 5 in the first innings, was still on 0 when he went for a quick single, injured a muscle in his back and retired hurt. He did not play again that season and, as far as competitive Australian cricket was concerned, was the end. But already he had done enough. He easily headed the national batting and the bowling for the season: 403 runs for an average of 80.60 and nineteen wickets at a cost of 14 runs each. New South Wales won their last game against Victoria and retained the Sheffield Shield without losing a match. In four seasons Miller had led New South Wales to three successive Shields, a feat unparalleled since the turn of the century when New South Wales had won it six successive times.

Yet when the team for England was announced Ian Johnson was again preferred as captain. The playboy had not been forgiven.

Miller was not really surprised. Later he wrote, 'I never seriously thought I would [be captain]. I'm impulsive; what's more, I've never been Bradman's pin-up and the Don rates high when it comes to policy matters in Australian cricket'.

Now there were no more worlds to conquer. At the beginning of the year he had been awarded the MBE 'for services to sport, especially Australian cricket' and already his all-round Test record was supreme: 2,723 runs in 75 innings for an average of 38.90, 147 wickets at a cost of 22 runs each and 35 catches. There seemed every incentive to retire. Miller had always wanted to retire while still on top, with his position in the team unquestioned, his place in the public's affection based on deeds rather than memories. For some years he had been associated with cricket journalism and now there were offers of full-time journalism in both England and Australia. Miller was keen to make the transition and acutely conscious of the timing of retirement. He wrote in *Cricket From The Grandstand*, published after his retirement, 'You must cash in at the right time . . . It is amazing how quickly personal reputations lose their value commercially'. As the SS *Himalaya* carrying the 1956 Australian team to England left Fremantle, Miller dug Lindwall in the ribs and said, 'Take a good look at this scene. It's the last time you'll see it as a player'. Lindwall was not amused.

Nostalgia was to be evident in much that he did that season. On the way out he rediscovered his boyhood game of quoits with cricket writer Crawford White and the first match at Arundel recreated the fading glories of country-house cricket. There was a duke in attendance, guardsmen's busbies on the branches of an oak and marquees and picnics in the sun. Bedser opened the bowling, Brown and Wright played, Lindwall bowled Hutton for a duck and Marlar bowled Miller for a duck. Off the field he had better luck. The Duke of Norfolk gave a party for the Australian cricketers in the Baron's Hall of Arundel Castle. His teenage daughters, Jane, Sarah, Mary and Anne were allowed to miss classes at their convent school at Woldingham and stay up to meet the cricketers. During dinner they appeared at the gallery of the dinner hall and Anne called out, 'Mr Miller', and threw down some sweets. The whole hall responded with cheers as Keith made the catch. The next morning the girls arrived early for breakfast, hoping to catch another glimpse of Mr Miller but found that as usual he was late for breakfast.

The wider season was also marked by change. One by one Miller's great adversaries and friends were leaving the stage. Bedser had played his last Test, Morris and Hutton had retired the previous winter and Compton's knee promised at best a temporary respite.

But the old problem remained. This time, it was definitely asserted, Miller was to be regarded as a batsman. The Australians were short of class batsmen with experience of English wickets and they had brought a quartet of fast bowlers: Lindwall, Crawford, Davidson and Archer. Pace, in fact, was considered to be the likely decider of the series with Tyson and Statham very much on Australian minds; and the series was expected to be close. While Australia were recording an impressive victory in the Caribbean – the first by a visiting side – England could only manage to edge out South Africa 3–2 at home.

Miller began the tour with his customary batting display. In his first match at Leicester – the second of the tour – he made

281 not out, hitting a six, a five and thirty-four fours. That was on 8 May. On 16 May the Australians began their match against Surrey, then in the middle of their historic sequence of seven championship wins in a row. They won the toss, batted and made steady progress, the first wicket reaching 62. Then at twenty past twelve Laker was brought on. When he left the crease at quarter past six his figures read: 46 – 18 – 88 –10. Miller, with 57 not out, was the only one who escaped. His innings on a wicket that aided spin, though not wickedly, was totally unlike anything he had ever played before. He came in at no. 5 and made 18 in two hours, using his pads and his reach effectively, if somewhat inelegantly, to keep out Laker. Then with the last man in and the Surrey crowd getting the jitters every time Lock bowled lest he deprive Laker, Miller made 36 out of 42 in half an hour, hitting Lock for 11 and 14 in successive overs. In the end Laker got his tenth wicket and Miller, with one of those instinctive gestures that always characterised his play, shook Laker by the hand, and then took off his adversary's cap and ruffled his hair.

But the duel had proved a searing experience and it left its mark on him. Laker's summer had begun, and Miller the batsman soon realised that he had no part to play in it. In the second innings he made 2, Lock took seven wickets and Surrey won easily. After that in successive innings he made 10, 6, 0 and 26. In the First Test there was Laker again. Miller was lbw to him in both innings, making 0 and 4. The reach that had once flown into the most thrilling of off-side strokes was now used for ungainly defence; there were long and often grotesque periods of pad play and wild, even rustic swings. Now, more often than not, he could be seen batting with a cap: his hair had always been a vital element of his game but the cricket of 1956 was not part of his character. When a girl admirer expressed a desire to see him bat he replied, 'You'd better come early'.

But if the cricketer was often unhappy, the man was to enjoy his most eventful season. This was his farewell to England and he was determined to live every moment of it. There is a primitive appeal about England–Australia matches that almost defies description. I have seen grown men, even

hardened journalists, otherwise quite sane and indulgent
towards defeats by other countries, grow apoplectic at the
very mention of the Australians. Miller had never been
subject to such emotions. English cricket had always felt a
special affection for him, even when he appeared irritatingly
impetuous. Now this affection was tinged by a certain
poignancy. There seemed to be genuine sorrow that in this his
last tour he had not come back as captain of his country.

He was now at the height of his considerable social powers.
Almost anything he did was news. The day the Australian
team arrived, Crawford White reported:

> Last night he hoped to be able to get to the Festival Hall for the
> Beethoven Choral Symphony instead of the lighter entertain-
> ment of the Coliseum (where the rest of the team went). Miller
> explained, 'It's not often I get a chance to hear such a great work
> as this, and I don't want to miss it'.

Lord Tedder provided him with a car for his exclusive use and
apart from the usual trips to the race courses there were three
significant social events, the most notable of which was
dinner with Princess Margaret at Lord Mountbatten's house
near Southampton – receiving the MBE and visiting Royal
Ascot were the others.

The dinner came while he was captaining the Australians
against Hampshire in late June. He had just had ten days off
cricket, during which he had been stuck on a Thames
mudbank while holidaying on Godfrey Evans's house-boat,
and had had his wallet, containing the invitation to the Palace
for the MBE ceremony, stolen while he was resting on
Brighton beach. He turned up late, missed the toss, and there
was general lethargy about the play when suddenly he
received the dinner invitation from Lord Mountbatten. It was
so unexpected that Miller, who had left most of his clothes in
London, went in his only available lounge suit which
considerably embarrassed him though it did not seem to affect
his hosts. He spent much of the evening watching a thriller
starring Edward G. Robinson and exchanging 'Who do you
think did it' with Princess Margaret.

The event was predictably front-page news and he spent the rest of the match deflecting newsmen's questions. Part of his exchange with Desmond Hackett went:

Hackett: What did you wear?
Miller: It was an informal occasion.
Hackett: Did you sit next to the Princess?
Miller: That is a question I am not prepared to answer.
Hackett: Did you talk with the Princess?
Miller: Naturally, the company was so small that the conversation moved round the table.
Hackett: Was there music and dancing?
Miller: It was an informal and entertaining occasion.
Hackett: When did you leave?
Miller: When the party terminated.

Desmond Hackett was very impressed: 'Keith Miller the diplomat, did I say? Miller the complete diplomat'.

Hackett was not the only one who failed to prise out the details of that dinner conversation. Even close friends were rebuffed by 'It was a private occasion'. But many years later Miller told a persistent Frank Rostron, 'Well, all the Princess said was, "Mr Miller, the butler did it"'.

Cricket increasingly appeared to be an interlude, and when it intervened it was in the familiar pattern for English tours. Miller had come as a batsman but he conquered, briefly, as a bowler, becoming the leading Australian bowler and achieving his best figures in three tours of England. His bowling figures for the series deserve a table all to themselves, so eloquent are they of his skill and effort in conditions that could not have been more daunting:

	Overs	Maidens	Runs	Wickets
First Test				
1st Innings	33	5	69	4
2nd Innings	19	2	58	2
Second Test				
1st Innings	34.1	9	72	5
2nd Innings	36	12	80	5

Third Test	Did not bowl because of fluid on the knee.			
Fourth Test				
1st Innings	21	6	41	0
	Australia lost by an innings.			
Fifth Test				
1st Innings	40	7	91	4
2nd Innings	22	3	56	1
Series	205.1	44	467	21

How were the circumstances daunting? Consider them. In two Tests there was no Lindwall (he finished with seven wickets at a cost of 34 runs each). Miller was playing under a captain he believed to be his inferior. And in this season of spinners this is what the two principal Australian spinners achieved in Tests:

	Overs	Maidens	Runs	Wickets
Johnson	119	31	303	6
Benaud	154	48	330	8

Of course Miller's bowling was mostly containment, designed to save matches, as it did in the First and Fifth Tests, rather than win them. But this did not involve any loss in one of the most essential features of his cricket: his search for quality. In the First, five of his six victims were established batsmen, in the Fourth, four of his five. And in between there had been his most complete triumph on English soil. It came appropriately at Lord's in the middle of June.

Up to this point the weather had matched Miller's cricketing mood: cold cutting winds at Worcester and Leicester, rain at Bradford and at Old Trafford, cold enough at Fenners for log fires to be a realistic speculation, leaden clouds at Hove and rain again at Trent Bridge. But as the Australians returned to London there was sunshine and the only hard wicket of the series. The day before the match, Miller visited Royal Ascot in grand style: grey topper and morning coat from Moss Bros, publicity photographs with a model and paragraphs in the society columns of the national newspapers.

In the Test, apart from the first innings where he made 28 not out out of 285, he played a decisive part at every stage of the match. In the first England innings, without Lindwall and Davidson and after Crawford had broken down after five overs, Miller, bowling generally at fast-medium and moving the ball either way, took the wickets of Richardson, Graveney, Watson, Trueman and Bailey: five for 72 in 34.1 overs. Australia led by 114 and their first-innings score even began to look match-winning.

Miller's main bowling effort had come on Saturday morning – always the high point of the season and in 1956 the only Test Saturday when the sun shone consistently. That very evening he produced a little gem of an innings as his batting farewell to Lord's. He came in at 5.30 and in the next fifty minutes he made 30 'imperial runs' (in the words of Rex Alston) out of 33, with three fours, seven twos. Nobody bowled a maiden, not even Bailey. Then at 6.20 Trueman came back, Miller hit a four and was out to the last ball. He left as he had come: Lord's ringing with warm, valedictory applause. But there was still a Test Match to be won.

England began the fifth day needing 300 to win, eight wickets in hand. They still had a good chance of forcing a draw, and Watson, who had thwarted the Australians in 1953, was still there. Fifteen minutes into the morning Miller bowled Watson and then in an hour after lunch he took the wickets of May, Evans and Wardle, to finish with five for 72 and ten for 172 in seventy overs in the match. Australia had won by 185 runs and led 1-0 in the series. As he led the victorious Australians off the field, Miller took a bail from umpire Frank Lee's breast pocket and with a broad, sweeping gesture tossed it into the crowd.

It is a measure of his achievements that now, even though this Australian team was generally considered to be their weakest since 1912, considerable doubts were being expressed about England's ability to retain the Ashes, with the batting felt to be particularly suspect. These doubts were

magnified when the selectors recalled Washbrook, himself a
selector, and there was wide public criticism. But Washbrook
proved a great success, the next two Tests provided turning
wickets, England had Laker and by the time the Australians
returned to London it was a very different story. They had
failed by humiliating margins to regain the Ashes and felt
embittered and angry.

After the first of these defeats in the Third Test at Leeds,
where Miller made 41 out of 143 and 26 out of 140, the
simmering disquiet over Johnson's captaincy escalated into an
open campaign by the Australian Press to have him replaced
by Miller. On the eve of the Fourth Test the selection
committee of Johnson, Langley and Miller met. Miller, aware
of the delicacy of Johnson's position and perhaps no longer
wanting the captaincy, decided to skirt the issue. He
suggested that Craig replace Burge, a suggestion which was
accepted. The captaincy was never discussed.

It is impossible to say what the effect of a Miller captaincy
would have been. Already the series had turned. He might
have managed to soften the margin of defeat but not, I think,
prevent it. By common consent few teams could have lived
with Laker and Lock that season, least of all the 1956
Australians, and the demand for a Miller captaincy was a
reflection more of the confusion and bewilderment that the
Australians felt than of positive hope of success.

This was emphasised in the next Test. The Australians had
one look at the Manchester wicket – it was bare of grass, it was
marled and at tea on the first day when the wicket was swept a
dust cloud erupted – and mentally hoisted the white flag.
Miller told Frank Lee: 'I think three days will see this
through'. In fact, rain was to drag it into the fifth day. England
won the toss and made 459. Then Laker came on and achieved
cricket's greatest Test bowling feat by taking 19 wickets.
Australia made 84 and 205, Miller falling to Laker both times
for 6 and 0 (see plate 11). The consequences were immediately
felt: a whole generation of Australians were convinced that
the English had 'cooked' the wicket. Their anger was directed
at one man: Gubby Allen, then Chairman of the selectors.

Gubby Allen told me:

> The Manchester wicket was definitely not cooked. While we were picking the team for the Manchester Test 'Washie' [Washbrook] told us that the Manchester wicket was going to be the best batting wicket of the series. On the day before the Test, stories started floating around and correspondents asked me if I had seen the wicket. Initially I dismissed these stories. But when I saw the wicket it looked funny. I pressed by fingers into it; the top had gone. The wicket will go by tea-time, I thought. I was about to call for the groundsman when Washie appeared. He was taken aback. 'This wicket has completely changed character.' Just then the Chairman of the Grounds Committee came up to me and said, 'Do you want any more grass cut off?' I said, 'It wouldn't break my heart, but ask the groundsman, not me. See rule 7.' This part of the story got around and everybody, particularly the Australians, said Gubby Allen was behind it. Actually what happened was that the groundsman put the marl on top only ten days before the match – far too late. When he started to water it a member objected and the top layer was not properly bound.

Even Miller was affected by the general bitterness that followed the disaster. After the Australian first innings Johnson tried to rally his men: we can fight back, we need guts, we can save the match. Miller detached himself from the race form he was studying and said, 'Bet you 6 to 4 we can't'. Such a negative, if realistic, remark must have further deepened the Australian gloom.

From now on, crowds came to match after match to record their affectionate farewell, though there was one moment of fright. At Birmingham there was a threat to shoot Miller if the Australians won. Miller made 46 not out and led the Australians to a superb innings victory. The threat never materialised.

The farewell was completed in the traditional manner at the Oval. The evening before the match Miller went on television and announced that he was retiring on his return to Australia. Though his intentions had been common knowledge in cricket circles, Australian officials affected surprise. Television appearances were forbidden in the players' contracts and the team had still to play four Tests in India and Pakistan. Miller's announcement caused a great deal of comment during the match and he later issued a statement seeking to retrieve his position.

For the Oval Test England had recalled Compton whose knee was once again operational. All the pre-match notices stressed that this was the last time the 'cavaliers' would be seen together and on the first day the nostalgia was complete. Compton was very nearly bowled by Miller's first ball but then in one of the half a dozen truly romantic innings of the modern age he went on to make 94 and even the Australians were sorry when he was out.

Miller's performances were less evocative but he almost certainly saved Australia from defeat with some of his best batting of the series. In the first innings he came in to bat when Australia were 47 to 5 and in considerable danger of instant annihilation. By the time he was out, nearly four hours later, Australia were only 45 behind England and for the first time Laker had been made to look somewhat human. It was not an innings of beauty. It could not be: this was still a difficult turning wicket. There were some spells of pad play, once a kick in the style of a hockey goal-keeper, but there were also some tremendous leg-side hits including two sixes.

In the second innings Australia were left 228 to make in two hours and Miller came in to bat when Australia were 5 for 3 with Harvey, the only other batsman likely to counter Laker and Lock, out. For the next seventy minutes he made 7 runs, protecting his fellow batsman from Laker, and Australia were safe. Then, as the sun and the rain appeared simultaneously, Miller, uncapped, his bat held aloft, left the English Test scene for the last time while the Oval responded with warm, loving applause. That was very nearly the end.

He played one further Test. In early October Australia played Pakistan at Karachi and in a match made notorious by the fact that only 95 runs were scored on the first day – the lowest total recorded in a single day's play – he made 32 and took two wickets. He did not play in India and returned to Australia to make his retirement official: 'Family reasons, future work, and a desire to retire before I am thrown out have brought about my retirement.'

13

Miller's cricket writings fall into two distinct phases: during his playing days he wrote the occasional piece of journalism mainly for the Associated Newspapers of Sydney and co-authored seven books with Richard Whitington; on retirement he took to full-time journalism with the *Daily Express*. The difference is not one of form alone. While his journalism followed a much-traversed post-war path, the books form a minor but unique segment of modern cricket writing. It is not that they contain any great writing. In fact, age has not been kind to them. Today, twenty years later, they have a certain period interest, nothing else. But they remain the products of the first and only public marriage between a cricketer still in his prime and a professional writer. By the time the first book – *Cricket Caravan* – was published in 1950, Miller's reputation was already secure and Whitington had established himself.

The books also followed a formula that had never been used and has never been repeated. They fed on the public image of Miller and in turn embellished it. The formula never varied. There would be a foreword by a famous personality, a likeness of Keith Miller on the cover and a neat division of subject matter. Duleepsinhji wrote the foreword for the third book, *Straight Hit*; Sir Robert Menzies for the fourth, *Bumper*; Sir John Barbirolli for the fifth, *Gods or Flannelled Fools?* and C. B. Fry wrote a guest chapter for the last one, *Cricket Typhoon*. Sir Robert had not even read the book, Sir John had read one chapter. The photographs of Miller were the ones that had graced a thousand newspapers: Miller just after he had delivered a ball, Miller finishing a cover-drive, Miller the

Brylcreemed hair prominent, staring challengingly at the reader.

The division of subject matter was, perhaps, a little too neat. The first half would contain essays on cricket subjects, mostly within a narrow groove: Bradman and his effect on the game, the rights and wrongs of the bumper, the greatest twentieth-century bowler, the greatest twentieth-century batsman, the need for more colour in cricket. The second half was filled with descriptive accounts of the Miller Test series. Between 1950 and 1955 Miller participated in six series and there were seven books, one of them an anthology of the earlier books.

The books appear to be largely the creation of Richard Whitington, and Miller was occasionally unaware of what Whitington was up to. *Bumper* was published in the early spring of 1953 to coincide with the Australian tour of England. In a chapter on the future of Australian cricket it said:

> Lindsay Hassett's captaincy has been too much influenced by an increasingly cautious outlook in recent years. Lindsay is apt to miss the recurring opportunity when it comes and is also apt to do nothing about it for fear that what steps he takes may prove to be the wrong ones . . . Lindsay is no lover of criticism. He was also schooled for summers under that most cautious, albeit wide-awake of captains, Bradman. But the great difference between the captaincy of Hassett and Bradman is that Bradman made his plans half-an-hour ahead of the changing plot of the game, whereas Hassett deals, or fails to deal, with things as they occur.

The day it was published the Australians were guests at a lunch of the Institute of Journalists. All the evening newspapers carried news about the book and one had a 72-point banner headline: KEITH MILLER CRITICISES HIS CAPTAIN.

All eyes were on Hassett as he rose to speak. He started introducing the players, then came Miller's turn. Hassett said, 'Keith, as you probably know, is a journalist. All the journalists in London tell me that he has published a book. I don't know anything about it.'

Neither did Miller. The chapter had been written by
Whitington and he had not even read it.

The books mined two extremely lucrative post-war seams.
There was a tremendous boom in cricket books, particularly
tour accounts – eighteen books covered the 1953 series in
England, ten books, three booklets and a pamphlet the
1954–55 MCC visit to Australia – and there was a growing
appetite for details of dressing-room gossip, for the anecdote
that promised to reveal but often proved to be superficial, for
tit-bits of character and conduct. Thus *Straight Hit*, primarily
an account of the 1951–52 West Indies tour to Australia,
contained the information that 'Sonny [Ramadhin] is a better
bowler on a full stomach than he is on an empty one' and that
'the West Indians arranged for Ramadhin to have lunch
before play started for the day, if and when he so desired it'.

In their discursive moods Miller and Whitington followed
a fairly consistent and unarguable line. They were for
brighter cricket, in favour of wickets that gave batsmen and
bowlers a chance, and against petty officialdom. Directed
largely at English audiences, obeisance to the mother country
was an almost constant theme, though in this they were
probably reflecting the temper of the times. The arguments
were straight talk from men who had been in the heat of the
kitchen and were meant to instruct. They occasionally
amused and almost invariably provoked controversy.

Straight Hit discussed Freddie Brown, England's captain in
the 1950–51 series: 'Brown disappointed many people who
came into close contact with him during the tour by his often
brusque, sometimes even downright rude behaviour towards
them'. When I asked Brown about it he said, 'Oh, it was so
long ago, I really can't remember'. In 1952 Brown's reactions
were stronger. He told the Press, 'The authors apparently
wrote this for sensationalism. I shall ignore it. Miller and I got
on well during the tour, I wish he would say these things to
me.'

Occasionally the books descended to juvenilia. *Gods or
Flannelled Fools?* began a chapter on Peter May thus: 'Peter
May (and we are sure he will)'. But on the whole the writing

managed to convey the gusto and delight of the authors. The introduction to *The Keith Miller Companion* puts it well:

> Cricket writing has taken us to such places as the Viceroy's Palace in New Delhi, where one of us inadvertently trod upon Marshal [*sic*] Wavell's toe, to the Palace of Perfumes in Cairo, where both of us inadvertently failed to detect that a certain perfume was Australian wattle, and to the Rand Club in Johannesburg where at least one of us inadvertently downed a pint of Tennant's beer.

The books became a regular feature of the cricket scene and for once the blurb writer was right: 'No season would now be complete without Miller and Whitington dispensing their own salty brand of comment and criticism'. They also earned praise. John Arlott found the standard of *Cricket Caravan* 'higher than that of most books by outstanding players' and the *Times Literary Supplement* recommended *Catch* to Test players.

But by 1956 the staccato style had begun to jar, the arguments had become repetitive and the formula jaded. The partnership was dissolved and has never been properly revived. It is not clear what exactly caused the breach. According to a journalist who was on the 1955 West Indian trip Whitington was upset when Miller, as Australian vice-captain, refused to discuss team selections with him. They did come together briefly in 1969 when Cassells published *Fours Galore*, an account of the 1968–69 West Indies tour of Australia. This book was different in shape and form from the earlier books and clearly segregated the work of the two authors. Whitington provided background details while Miller described the Australian-West Indies Tests. *British Books In Print* treated it as a book by Whitington.

There followed two books by Keith Miller 'alone'. In 1956 Miller, while on tour, arranged to publish his autobiography. He would talk to Reg Hayter, who runs one of Fleet Street's most successful sports news services and is now editor of *The Cricketer*, over convivial drinks in bars up and down the country. Hayter would convey the notes to Basil Easterbrook and Easterbrook would actually write the book. Easterbrook says, 'It is the hardest thing I ever did. Every time I was short of material Hayter would have another talk with Keith Miller and I would get some more copy.' He finally finished it on holiday. The book does not mention Easterbrook's name, though Miller did inscribe a copy 'To Bas, for all his help'. The *Daily Express* serialised it while Miller was still under contract not to write on cricket and the Australian Board of Control fined Miller £100. He appealed, lost, and finally accepted the offer of a Melbourne confectionery firm to pay the fine.

Naturally, the book was different from the Miller–Whitington books. The first few chapters were autobiographical and contained the only serious details about his early childhood that have been committed to print until now. There were chapters on the personalities of the game such as Bradman and Hassett and there were discussions of Miller interests like racing, royalty and music. Three years later Miller published *Cricket From The Grandstand*. This resurrected the formula: discussions on topical aspects of the game followed by a record of the 1958–59 MCC visit to Australia.

Since then Miller has continued to write for the *Daily Express*. Other newspapers were also interested in obtaining what was considered a 'prize catch'. In 1956, as news of his retirement leaked, Charles Bray made a bid to secure him for his own paper, the *Daily Herald*. But over a pleasant lunch at the Savoy, Miller told Bray that he did not want a public auction of his talents, and in the end he decided on the *Express* whose owners were already his friends. Max Aitken, son of Lord Beaverbrook, was a colleague from his war-time flying days and the *Express* offer of £25,000 spread over a number of years was a very good one. So every summer until 1974, when he took up a full-time post with Vernons Pools in Australia, the *Express* brought Miller over to England and used him as their expert. In this he was one of a proliferating band of ex-cricketers who had turned expert, a migration almost as old as the game itself. On 18 May 1904 *Punch* printed a cartoon of two batsmen running between wickets with their bats under their arms, busy scribbling away. The caption read; 'Spoiling Sport (a number of our cricketers have turned to writing)'. It neatly summed up the views of *Punch* about cricketers such as C. B. Fry, A. O. Jones, A. C. Maclaren, J. T. Tyldesley, T. W. Hayward, Ranjitsinhji, P. F. Warner, the Australian Alan Marshall and Gilbert Jessop who were then writing about the game.

The communications boom after the Second World War institutionalised the process. Major newspapers started sending their correspondents to cover Test matches, with many of them following the sun all the year round. Television changed the style of journalistic reporting: tele-pictures preceded the word report, analysis replaced description, and comment, rather than news, became sacred. In the continuing and ruthless war of circulation between the popular Fleet Street dailies the success formula of 'crime, cricket and crumpet' acquired a new edge. The hiring of a 'name' became a badge of editorial virility.

Alex Bannister, doyen of the Fleet Street cricket journalists, calls it 'copy cat journalism. If my major competitor has the England opening batsman, then I must secure the England opening bowler'. The next step was almost inevitable: the ghost became indispensable. He is usually a competent and knowledgeable journalist but not sufficiently well known to make an attractive and immediately recognisable by-line.

The method of operation is simple. The ghost and the name both watch the match, they discuss aspects of a day's play, decide on an angle with the paper's regular correspondent, who usually writes the weightier, descriptive stuff, and then the ghost writes the story. It is by no means simple. The style must be in consonance with the cricketer's personality and his playing image, yet the accent must be on startling originality. Here is a quotation, entirely representative, from Miller's 'ghosted' *Cricket From The Grandstand*:

> Sheer bunkum! That's how I feel about the so-called amateurism in English County Cricket. Peter May, Colin Cowdrey, Trevor Bailey and the rest may not receive direct payment for playing, but believe me, they're not short of a pound or two during the season. They get their cuts indirectly from the game.

This is a necessary prelude to any discussion about Miller's journalism, for it emphasises how greatly it was to his credit that he always wrote his own stories for the *Daily Express*.

Miller has always been quick to react to any slight to his journalistic ability. E. M. Wellings in his book, *The Ashes Thrown Away*, made some characteristically pungent remarks about how Miller had received help from another journalist while covering the 1958–59 MCC tour to Australia. Miller's reply was equally robust: 'Let me be frank. In common with many other pressmen, I did have assistance not unusual in the covering of an important sporting event. Mr Wellings often has assistance (unpaid) himself; when a little bemused on the finer points of the game he has asked my opinion of an incident and subsequently used that opinion as his own expert criticism. I would like Mr Wellings to know that I have been top-graded in the Australian Journalists' Association for over ten years, that I was Australia's first sporting columnist, and that I am still under contract to write a weekly sporting column that is distributed throughout Australia. Nevertheless I am not too proud to ask another journalist for help on certain aspects of stylised writing. After all, practically every journalist copy goes through the helping hand of sub-editor before it is published. I'll admit that I know more about cricket than the mechanics of journalism just as Mr Wellings knows more about the mechanics of journalism than about cricket. I am always willing to help Mr Wellings and any other journalist who asks my help on technical cricket points, and despite Mr Wellings ill-natured remarks I shall continue to do so.'

Miller was aware that migration to the press box meant a change in his previous rôle. He wrote:

> I always tried to soft pedal about chaps I was playing with or against . . . Dick wrote the stronger comment, and touched upon the subjects that were taboo to me. You can't knock 'em when you have a common goal and you do have this when you walk on to the same cricket field. It's different on retirement. Then you are free to have a go.

Miller had chosen the right vehicle for his views. The *Daily Express* has always had a reputation for being associated with famous personalities. Its style of journalism, with its flavour of hardened men of the world possessing an unerring anticipation for immediate news and fearless ability to interpret it, and fully conscious of the need to preserve the values that made Britain great, matched Miller's public image. The *Express*'s use of him has been characteristic. Within days of Miller's last Test at the Oval the *Daily Express* declared in banner headlines: KEITH MILLER DECLARES! READ HIS STORY IN THE EXPRESS NEXT WEEK – IT'S A HONEY and almost nine years later on 27 May 1965 the paper's trailer showed a photograph of Miller above this headline:

See who's here . . . *Keith Miller*
Fresh from covering the exciting series between West Indies and Australia. Today he's at Edgbaston for the first Test between England and New Zealand. How do England compare with the world champions? What does he think of Freddie Trueman's return? Read his expert comments in the *Daily Express* tomorrow.

And expert was what he was. While Crawford White, the newspaper's regular correspondent till recently, concentrated on the routine aspects of a day's play, Miller chose an angle and attacked. Consider this comment the day after India won their first Test on English soil at the Oval in 1971. Under the headline 'Patch up the gaps this way England' he wrote:

The selectors must scrap the crazy notion that opening batsmen must only play as openers. Good batsmen can bat in any position. So now I put forward the names of the men I would select to face the Aussies, and all have made their names as opening batsmen. They are Boycott, Roy Virgin, Mike Denness, Brian Luckhurst, John Edrich and Jameson . . . England's bowling is top class – make no mistake and Ray Illingworth has shown when the chips are down he is still their best spinner.

Miller's writing has been, like his cricket, full of commitment. He has espoused the cause of unfashionable batsmen, spelt out the problems for bowlers who are over the hill and always been free with advice on the cures for the many ills of English cricket. Nor has he allowed the press box – which for a cricketer turned writer can often be an alien place – to intimidate him.

Lord's has probably the best appointed press box in the country. It has a bar of its own, it is spacious and it has a certain sense of serenity. But it has a very, very small entrance: guests have to be signed for on match days and they are only allowed in after lunch – even then they are not very welcome. This is wholly understandable. There is a job to be done and outsiders, however well meaning, can be an intrusion. Once Miller entered the press box with a few friends, including some ladies. E. W. Swanton, who in later years had employed a lady secretary to help him with his cricket work, was upset over the presence of strange ladies and remonstrated. Miller was quick with his retort: 'You were the first to introduce ladies into the press box, and anyway, Swanton, you're occupying my bloody seat'.

But Miller has not found it easy to play the rôle of the expert. Godfrey Evans explains it well:

> People are always coming up to you, asking for autographs, disturbing you. You need to get away. So whenever Keith and I reported on Tests at Nottingham we would go to a nearby hotel. I was very friendly with the manager there and he would book us into a room. Here we would follow the play on television. If there was racing on the other channel we would switch over and Keith would ring up his bookie and lay a bet. We would watch the play in comfort, have a quiet drink.

Journalism does not appear to have changed the man. He is still easily bored and he has never allowed the conformist call of prosaic duty to interfere with loyalties to friends. Jean Bowler, Miller's good friend from RAF days and now a London housewife, recalls:

> I worked for a Mr Seal for many years – dear old soul. The old

man had a bar in the boardroom and Dusty would often come to the office to have a chat, a few drinks. One day, this was in 1970, I rang Dusty: the old man is dying. He was supposed to be covering some important championship match. It was some match against Essex, I think. He missed it and came to the office. We talked of old times, drank, the old man was really happy. That was on August 2nd. On August 22nd the old man was dead.

But what value are we to place on Miller's writing? While the cricketer's place in history is not open to debate, the journalist is in a very different position. This sort of writing has become so voluminous in recent years and its influence is so uncertain that a proper historical view cannot yet be formed. It has in part contributed to the stagnation in Fleet Street cricket writing, and here we are faced with a problem of possible bias. No major cricket writer has been promoted by the national newspapers in the last few years, it being more attractive and cheaper to hire an expert on contract rather than to blood a youngster. This is something that concerns all working journalists and Alex Bannister probably sums up the view of most of them:

> These experts are spoiling the market for the others. They are no journalists – the mere writing of articles does not make one a journalist. You have to go through the mill, then develop specialisation. Anyway, no cricketer I have known was able to write well.

This may appear unduly harsh. Quite a few ex-cricketers have proved themselves to be competent writers though none, Jack Fingleton apart, has gone through the Bannister routine. But then Fingleton is a special case: he was a journalist long before he became a Test cricketer and rightly resents being called a cricketer turned writer.

For a definitive view of Miller the journalist, let us go back to that mild winter day in February 1975, the flat in Baker Street and Sir Neville Cardus. For very nearly three hours he talked about Miller, glowing after every reminiscence. I asked him about Miller the journalist. 'Keith, a writer?' He smiled, shook his head and said, 'Arthur Mailey could write, and of course Jack Fingleton. Don Bradman, if he wants to – but then he always could do anything if he applied himself. None of the others'.

.   .   .

Jet-set cricket became firmly established soon after Miller's retirement from the first-class game – the sun never sets on the cricket commonwealth – and he often played festival matches in many parts of the world. In 1958 he played in aid of the Pakistan Flood Relief Fund. In 1959 he was made a member of MCC and in return he decided to play a few matches for the Club. In preparation for this he appeared for Nottingham-shire against Cambridge University, made 62 and 102 not out and took two wickets for 35 in the first innings but could not bowl in the second. But even this brief presence had an effect on crowds. Nottinghamshire that season were bottom of the table attracting no more than 1,000 spectators for their non-championship matches. 5,000 turned up to see Miller and were vastly amused when he waved his bat in mock anger at a bowler who had sent down a couple of bouncers. The week after that he played for MCC against Oxford University, took one wicket, but when he began to bat he tore his calf muscle. That was the end as far as the record books went.

But Miller, to this day, has continued to play cricket in some form or other. There were fun and frolic afternoon games – some six of them – between the *Daily Express* and the *Daily Mail*, in one of which Miller scored 87 in between phoning bets on Ascot races, and in November 1976 a startled cricket public were told that Keith Miller was making a cricket comeback. He had decided to captain an international XI in seven one-day games across the length and breadth of Pakistan between 21 November and 5 December 1976. They were part of the Pakistani celebrations in honour of the centenary of their founder, Mohammed Ali Jinnah. Ian Wooldridge met Miller just before he set off to Pakistan and found him both unprepared and angry. He had no pads, an undersized bat borrowed from somebody else and no shoes but he was determined to play because otherwise Australia would be the only cricketing country to go unrepresented.

'I need another game of cricket like I need a bullet through the brain,' he said. 'It's simply because I am disgusted at the way four of our present star Australian Test players knocked back invitations to play in some celebration games in Pakistan. It means that the only country who wouldn't be represented there was Australia. That's rude and that's undiplomatic and it's because our players get so much money these days that they just don't give a damn and for once in my life I'm going to get off my ass and do something about it.'

The gesture once again showed Miller's penchant for making the right move, though the cricket was largely meaningless. As Miller had said often enough, he wanted to be remembered as a Test cricketer, and he will be.

When a great cricketer retires he leaves behind a whole host of memories. They are generally inextricably linked with his cricket deeds. These provoke discussion, produce awe and, in moments of sadness, provide consolation. Miller's figures will always proclaim his greatness but they will never reveal the man who went beyond those figures to become a legend in his own playing days. Nor, of course, the man who even today, more than twenty years after his retirement, remains a considerable and potent public figure.

A few years ago one of Miller's grown sons travelled with him to England. A crowd of friends, many of them beautiful women, had assembled at Heathrow to greet Miller. His son was staggered, and probably pleased, at this first-hand experience of the legend. Miller took him to one side and said, 'Son, there are a lot of things in life which you'll have time enough to learn about. But this is where we part. You go your way, I'll go mine.'

Statistical Appendix

Figures and records mean little to Keith Miller. But since this is a
cricketing biography here they are. And they tell their own
remarkable story.

I. The All-rounder: (All First-class Matches)

Season	I.	N.O.	Batting Runs	H.S.	Avge	Bowling Runs	Wkts	Avge
1937–38 (Australia)	1	0	181	181	181.00	—	—	—
1938–39 (Australia)	7	2	125	55	25.00	—	—	—
1939–40 (Australia)	11	1	298	108	29.80	—	—	—
1940–41 (Australia)	5	0	140	63	28.00	27	1	27.00
1945 (England)	13	3	725	185	72.50	336	10	33.60
1945–46 (India)	14	1	470	132	36.15	343	13	26.38
1945–46 (Australia)	9	1	463	105*	57.87	191	6	31.83
1945–46 (New Zealand)	4	0	257	139	64.25	27	5	5.40
1946–47 (Australia)	19	3	1202	206*	75.12	725	32	22.65
1947–48 (Australia)	17	0	791	170	46.52	940	33	28.48
1948 (England)	26	3	1088	202*	47.30	985	56	17.58
1948–49 (Australia)	13	1	400	109	33.33	265	11	24.09
1949–50 (Australia)	4	0	107	80	26.75	121	8	15.12
1949–50 (South Africa)	18	3	577	131	38.46	728	44	16.54
1950–51 (Australia)	20	3	1332	214	78.35	762	27	28.22
1951–52 (Australia)	17	1	584	129	36.50	680	32	21.25
1951–52 (Ceylon)	1	0	106	106	106.00	24	5	4.80
1952–53 (Australia)	17	0	558	108	32.82	684	34	20.11
1953 (England)	31	3	1433	262*	51.17	1013	45	22.51
1953–54 (Australia)	12	2	711	143	71.10	540	16	33.75
1954–55 (Australia)	12	0	381	86	31.75	489	19	25.73
1955 (West Indies)	11	0	577	147	52.45	791	26	30.42
1955–56 (Australia)	10	1	638	164	70.88	272	19	14.31
1956 (England)	29	6	843	281*	36.65	980	50	19.60
1956 (Pakistan)	2	0	32	21	16.00	58	2	29.00
1959 (England)	3	2	164	102*	164.00	87	3	29.00
TOTAL	326	36	14,183	281*	48.90	11,068	497	22.26

Fielding. Miller took 129 catches in his career.

II. *The Batsman*

(a) *Where Miller Scored his Runs*

	Innings	Not Out	Runs	Highest Score	Average
In Australia	174	15	7911	214	49.75
In England	102	17	4253	281*	50.03
In South Africa	18	3	577	131	38.46
In India	14	1	470	132	36.15
In West Indies	11	0	577	131	52.45
In New Zealand	4	0	257	133	64.25
In Ceylon	1	0	106	106	106.00
In Pakistan	2	0	32	21	16.00
TOTAL	326	36	14,183	281*	48.90

(b) *Teams for whom Miller Scored his Runs*

	Innings	Not Out	Runs	Highest Score	Average
For Australia and Australian Touring Teams	165	19	6401	281*	43.84
For Victoria	30	4	1411	206*	54.26
For New South Wales	57	6	2838	214	55.64
For Australian Services	36	2	1352	132	39.76
For Australian XI	10	0	449	106	44.90
For Miscellaneous XI's	28	5	1732	185	75.30
TOTAL	326	36	14,183	281*	48.90

(c) The Miller Centuries

1937–38	181	Victoria v. Tasmania at Melbourne
1939–40	108	Victoria v. South Australia at Melbourne
1945	185	The Dominions v. England at Lord's
1945	105	Australia v. England at Lord's (Victory Test)
1945	118	Australia v. England at Lord's (Victory Test)
1945–46	106	Australian Services v. West Zone at Bombay
1945–46	132	Australian Services v. Ceylon at Colombo
1945–46	105*	Australian Services v. New South Wales at Sydney
1945–46	139	Australia v. Auckland at Auckland
1946–47	188	Victoria v. South Australia at Adelaide
1946–47	153	Victoria v. New South Wales at Melbourne
1946–47	206*	Victoria v. New South Wales at Sydney
1946–47	141*	Australia v. England at Adelaide
1947–48	170	New South Wales v. West Australia at Sydney
1948	202*	Australia v. Leicestershire at Leicester
1948	163	Australia v. MCC at Lord's
1948–49	109	New South Wales v. Queensland at Brisbane
1949–50	131	Australia v. Eastern Province at Port Elizabeth
1950–51	202*	New South Wales v. Queensland at Brisbane
1950–51	138*	New South Wales v. Queensland at Sydney
1950–51	122	New South Wales v. South Australia at Sydney
1950–51	214	New South Wales v. MCC at Sydney
1950–51	145*	Australia v. England at Sydney
1951–52	129	Australia v. West Indies at Sydney
1951–52	106	Commonwealth XI v. MCC at Colombo
1952–53	108	New South Wales v. Queensland at Brisbane
1953	262*	Australia v. Combined Services at Kingston
1953	220*	Australia v. Worcestershire at Worcester
1953	159*	Australia v. Yorkshire at Bradford
1953	109	Australia v. England at Lord's
1953–54 {	100 101 }	Hassett's XI v. Morris's XI at Melbourne
1953–54	143	New South Wales v. Victoria at Sydney
1955	147	Australia v. West Indies at Kingston
1955	137	Australia v. West Indies at Bridgetown
1955	109	Australia v. West Indies at Kingston
1955–56	164	New South Wales v. Queensland at Brisbane
1955–56	128	New South Wales v. West Australia at Perth
1955–56	106	Australian XI v. Tasmania at Hobart
1955–56	132	Governor-General's XI v. Prime Minister's XI at Karachi
1956	281*	Australia v. Leicestershire at Leicester
1959	102*	Nottinghamshire v. Cambridge University at Nottingham

(d) Notable Miller Partnerships

225 for the 1st wkt with Arthur Morris, New South Wales v. Queensland at Sydney, 1950–51

265 for the 2nd wkt with Arthur Morris, New South Wales v. MCC at Sydney, 1950–51

224 for the 3rd wkt with Neil Harvey, Australians v. West Indies at Kingston, 1955

206 for the 4th wkt with Ken Meelman, Victoria v. New South Wales at Sydney, 1946–47

207 for the 4th wkt with C. I. Gunasekara, Commonwealth XI v. MCC at Colombo, 1951–52

224 for the 4th wkt with Lindsay Hassett, Victoria v. South Australia at Adelaide, 1946–47

235 for the 4th wkt with Lindsay Hassett, Australia v. West Indies at Sydney, 1951–52

377 for the 4th wkt with Jim de Courcy, Australia v. Combined Services at Kingston, 1953

220 for the 5th wkt with Ron Archer, Australia v. West Indies at Kingston, 1955

204 for the 6th wkt with Ron Archer, Australia v. Leicestershire, Leicester 1956

206 for the 6th wkt with Ron Archer, Australia v. West Indies, Bridgetown, 1955

III. *The Bowler (All First-class Matches)*

Remarkable analyses

7 wkts for 12 runs	New South Wales v. South Australia 1955–56
7 wkts for 60 runs	Australia v. England, Brisbane 1946–47
6 wkts for 35 runs	Australia v. Natal, Pietermaritzburg 1949–50
5 wkts for 25 runs	Australia v. Hampshire, Southampton 1948
5 wkts for 26 runs	Australia v. West Indies, Sydney 1951–52
5 wkts for 29 runs	Australia v. Derbyshire, Derby 1956
5 wkts for 38 runs	New South Wales v. Victoria, Sydney 1954–55

IV. *The Test All-rounder*

(a) Batting

Tests	Innings	N.O.	Runs	H.S.	Avg.	100's	50's
55	87	7	2958	147	36.97	7	13

(b) Bowling

Tests	Balls	Mdns	Runs	Wkts.	Avg	5 Wkts Innings	10 Wkts Match
55	10,474	338	3905	170	22.97	7	1

(c) Fielding

Miller took 35 catches in Tests.

V. *The Test Batsman*

(a) How he made his Test runs

Opponents	Tests	Innings	N.O.	Runs	H.S.	Avg
England	29	49	4	1511	145*	33.57
India	5	5	0	185	67	37.00
New Zealand	1	1	0	30	30	30.00
Pakistan	1	2	0	32	21	16.00
South Africa	9	14	2	399	84	33.25
West Indies	10	16	1	801	147	53.40
TOTAL	55	87	7	2958	147	36.97

(b) How Miller Got Out in Tests

Season	Opponents	B	C	Lbw	St	Hit Wkt	Run Out	Not Out	Total
1946	New Zealand	—	1	—	—	—	—	—	1
1946–47	England	—	4	1	—	—	—	2	7
1947–48	India	1	2	2	—	—	—	—	5
1948	England	—	3	2	1	—	—	—	6
1949–50	South Africa	4	1	1	—	—	—	2	8
1950–51	England	2	5	1	—	—	—	1	9
1951–52	West Indies	4	3	1	—	1	—	1	10
1952–53	South Africa	2	2	2	—	—	—	—	6
1953	England	3	5	1	1	—	—	—	10
1954–55	England	3	3	—	—	—	1	—	7
1955	West Indies	—	3	2	—	—	1	—	6
1956	England	3	4	2	—	—	—	1	10
1956	Pakistan	1	1	—	—	—	—	—	2
	TOTAL	23	37	15	2	1	2	7	87

Career: 290 Completed innings; Bowled 76 times; Lbw 43; Caught 145; Stumped 13; Run Out 11; Hit Wicket 2.

(c) Bowlers who Dismissed Miller in Tests

			Total
1. *Spinners:*	Wright	6	
	Mankad	1	
	Laker	9	
	Holmes	1	
	Tayfield	1	
	Mann	2	
	Valentine	4	
	Wardle	4	
	Appleyard	1	
	Sobers	1	
			30
2. *Medium Fast:*	Smith	1	
	Yardley	2	
	Amarnath	1	
	Phadkar	2	
	Rangachari	1	
	Bedser	3	
	Pollard	1	
	Watkins	2	
	Mells	1	
	Bailey	4	
	Brown	3	
	Atkinson	2	
	Walcott	1	
	Worrell	3	
	Gomez	1	
	Trim	1	
	Fazal Mohammed	1	
	Khan Mohammed	1	
			31
3. *Fast*	Statham	3	
	Tyson	1	
	Trueman	2	
			6
			67
Others			11
Run Out			2
			80

VI. *The Test Bowler*

(a) How he took his Test wickets

Opponents	Runs	Wkts	Avg
England	1,949	87	22.40
India	223	9	24.77
New Zealand	6	2	3.00
Pakistan	58	2	29.00
South Africa	631	30	21.03
West Indies	1,038	40	25.95
Total	3,905	170	22.97

(b) Quality Analysis of Miller's Test wickets

Season	Opponents	Total	Batting Order										
			1.	2.	3.	4.	5.	6.	7.	8.	9.	10.	11.
1945–46	New Zealand	2	1	—	1	—	—	—	—	—	—	—	—
1946–47	England	16	3	2	1	1	1	2	—	3	—	2	1
1947–48	India	9	—	2	2	2	—	—	—	2	1	—	—
1948	England	13	3	2	—	3	2	—	1	—	2	—	—
1949–50	South Africa	17	3	2	1	2	2	2	1	2	2	—	—
1950–51	England	17	2	1	1	—	6	1	2	2	—	1	1
1951–52	West Indies	20	2	2	1	1	2	3	4	1	1	—	3
1952–53	South Africa	13	1	2	1	2	1	2	1	2	1	—	—
1953	England	10	—	1	3	—	1	2	—	1	1	1	—
1954–55	England	10	3	3	—	—	3	—	1	—	—	—	—
1955	West Indies	20	3	2	2	1	2	2	2	2	2	1	1
1956	England	21	3	1	4	3	2	1	2	1	3	1	—
1956	Pakistan	2	1	—	—	—	1	—	—	—	—	—	—
	Total	170	25	20	17	15	23	15	14	16	13	6	6

Of the 170 Test batsmen who fell to Miller, 47 were bowled, 16 lbw, 101 caught, 4 caught and bowled, and there were 2 hit wickets.

(c) Miller and Lindwall's Test record as a pair

Season	Opponents	Total wkts all bowlers	Lindwall	Miller	Pair	%
1945–46	New Zealand	20	2	2	4	20.0
1946–47	England	92	18	16	34	36.9
1947–48	India	95	18	9	27	28.4
1948	England	89	27	13	40	44.9
1949–50	South Africa	88	12	17	29	32.9
1950–51	England	83	15	17	32	38.5
1951–52	West Indies	89	21	20	41	46.0
1952–53	South Africa	86	19	13	32	37.2
1953	England	67	26	10	36	53.7
1954–55	England	81	14	10	24	29.6
1955	West Indies	86	20	20	40	46.5
1956	England	63	7	21	28	44.4
1956	Pakistan	11	1	2	3	27.2
	Total	950	200	170	370	38.9

[Lindwall took a further 28 wickets in nine more Tests to finish with 228 Test wickets before his retirement in 1959.]

Bibliography

BOOKS

Altham, H. S. and Swanton, E. W. *A History of Cricket* (London, George Allen &
    Unwin, 1962, 2 vols)
Alston, Rex:
    Taking The Air (London, Stanley Paul, 1951)
    Over to Rex Alston (London, Frederick Muller, 1953)
    Test Commentary (London, Stanley Paul, 1956)
Arlott, John:
    Gone To The Test Match (London, Longmans Green, 1949)
    Test Match Diary, 1953 (London, James Barrie, 1953)
    Australian Test Journal (London, Phoenix House, 1955)
    (Editor) *Cricket – The Great Allrounders* (London, Pelham Books, 1969)
Bailey, Trevor: *The Greatest of My Time* (London, Eyre & Spottiswoode, 1968)
Barker, Ralph and Rosenwater, Irving, *England v. Australia: A Compendium of Test
    Cricket between the Countries 1877–1968* (London, Batsford, 1969)
Barnes, Sidney:
    It Isn't Cricket (London, William Kimber, 1953)
    Eyes on the Ashes (London, William Kimber, 1953)
    The Ashes Ablaze (London, William Kimber, 1955)
Batchelor, Denzil:
    Days Without Sunset (London, Eyre & Spottiswoode, 1949)
    The Book of Tests (London, Hulton Press, 1953)
    The Picture Post Book of Tests (London, Hulton Press, 1955)
    Great Cricketers (London, Eyre & Spottiswoode, 1970)
Bedser, Alec & Eric:
    Our Cricket Story (London, Evans 1951)
    Following On (London, Evans, 1954)
Bedser, Alec (Editor): *Meet The Test Stars* (London, Charles Buchan, 1953)
Bradman, Sir Donald: *Farewell To Cricket* (London, Hodder & Stoughton, 1950)
Brodribb, Gerald: *Hit For Six* (London, Heinemann, 1960)
Brown, F. R.: *Cricket Crusader* (London, Nicholas Kaye, 1954)
Cardus, Neville:
    Cardus on Cricket (London, Souvenir Press, 1977)
    Cardus in the Covers (London, Souvenir Press, 1978)
Cary, Cliff; *Cricket Controversy* (London, Werner Laurie, 1948)
Compton, Denis:
    'Testing Time' For England (London, Stanley Paul, 1947)
    Playing For England (London, Sampson Low, Marston, 1948)
    In Sun & Shadow (London, Stanley Paul, 1952)
    End Of An Innings (London, Oldbourne Press, 1958)

Cutler, Norman:
  Behind The Tests (London, Putman, 1953)
  Behind The Australian Tests 1956 (London, Putman, 1956)
Dale, Harold: *Cricket Crusaders* (London, Werner Laurie, 1952)
Davidson, Alan: *Fifteen Paces* (London, Souvenir Press, 1963)
Dollery, H. E.: *Professional Captain* (London, Stanley Paul, 1952)
Edrich, W. J.:
  Cricket Heritage (London, Stanley Paul, n.d.)
  Cricketing Days (London, Stanley Paul, 1950)
  Round The Wicket (London, Frederick Muller, 1959)
Evans, Godfrey:
  Behind The Stumps (London, Hodder & Stoughton, 1951)
  Action In Cricket (London, Hodder & Stoughton, 1956)
  The Gloves Are Off (London, Hodder & Stoughton, 1960)
Ferguson, W. H.: *Mr Cricket* (London, Nicholas Kaye, 1957)
Fingleton, J. H.:
  Brightly Fades The Don (London, Collins, 1949)
  Brown and Company (London, Collins, 1952)
  The Ashes Crown The Year (London, Collins, 1954)
  Masters Of Cricket (London, Heinemann, 1958)
  Fingleton On Cricket (London, Collins, 1972)
Frith, David: *England Versus Australia: A Pictorial History of the Test Matches Since 1877*
  (London, Lutterworth/Smart, 1978)
Gilligan, A. E. R.:
  The Urn Returns (London, Deutsch, 1955)
  The Australian Challenge (London, Abelard-Schuman, 1956)
Gregory, Kenneth (compiler): *In Celebration of Cricket* (London, Hart Davis,
  MacGibbon, 1978)
Hammond, W. R.:
  Cricket My World (London, Stanley Paul, 1947)
  Cricket's Secret History (London, Stanley Paul, 1952)
Harris, Bruce:
  With England In Australia (London, Hutchinson, 1947)
  In Quest of the Ashes (London, Hutchinson, 1951)
  Cricket Triumph 1953 (London, Hutchinson, 1953)
  Ashes Triumphant 1954–55 (London, Hutchinson, 1956)
  Defending The Ashes (London, Hutchinson, 1956)
Harvey, Neil: *My World of Cricket* (London, Hodder & Stoughton, 1963)
Hughes, Margaret: *The Long Hop* (London, Stanley Paul, 1955)
Hutton, Len:
  Cricket is My Life (London, Hutchinson, 1953)
  Just My Story (London, Hutchinson, 1956)
Johnson, Ian: *Cricket at the Crossroads* (London, Cassell, 1957)
Kay, John:
  Ashes to Hassett (Altrincham, John Sherratt, 1951)
  Ducks and Hundreds (Altrincham, John Sherratt, 1949)
Kilburn, J. M.: *Thanks to Cricket* (London, Stanley Paul, 1972)
Laker, Jim: *Spinning Round the World* (London, Frederick Muller, 1957)
Landsberg, Pat: *The Kangaroo Conquers* (London, Museum Press, 1955)
Landsberg, Pat and Morris, Arthur: *Operation Ashes* (London, Robert Hale, 1956)

Lester, R.: *The Fight for the Ashes 1953* (London, Flagstaff Press, 1953)
Miller, Keith, and Whitington, R. S.:
  Cricket Caravan (London, Latimer, 1950)
  Catch (London, Latimer, 1951)
  Straight Hit (London, Latimer, 1952)
  Bumper (London, Latimer, 1953)
  Gods or Flannelled Fools? (London, Macdonald, 1954)
  The Keith Miller Companion (London, the Sportsman's Book Club, 1955)
  Cricket Typhoon (London, Macdonald, 1955)
Miller, Keith:
  Cricket Crossfire (London, Oldbourne Press, 1956)
  Cricket From The Grandstand (London, Oldbourne Press, 1959)
Moyes, A. G.:
  The Fight for the Ashes 1950–51 (London, Harrap, 1951)
  With the West Indies in Australia, 1951–52 (London, Harrap, 1952)
  The South Africans in Australia 1952–53 (London, Harrap, 1953)
  Australian Bowlers (London, Harrap, 1953)
  Australian Batsmen (London, Harrap, 1954)
  The Fight for the Ashes 1954–55 (London, Harrap 1955)
  Australian Cricket – A History (Sydney, Angus & Robertson, 1959)
O'Reilly, W. J.:
  Cricket Conquest (London, Werner Laurie, 1949)
  Cricket Task-Force (London, Werner Laurie, 1952)
Pollard, Jack:
  Six & Out: The Legend of Australian Cricket (Sydney, Angus & Robertson, 1965)
  Bumpers, Boseys and Brickbats (London, Murray, 1969)
Pollard, Jack (Editor): *Cricket the Australian Way* (London, Kaye 1961); 2nd edn
  Feltham, Newnes, 1969)
Robertson-Glasgow, R. C.: *More Cricket Prints* (London, Werner Laurie, 1949)
Robinson, Ray: *From the Boundary* (London, Collins, 1951)
Rosenwater, Irving: *Sir Donald Bradman* (London, Batsford, 1978)
Ross, Alan:
  Australia 55 (London, Michael Joseph, 1955)
  Cape Summer and the Australians in England (London, Hamish Hamilton, 1957)
Ross, Gordon: *Cricketers from Australia 1956* (London, Playfair, 1956)
Sarjeant, Sir David: *Australia, its cricket bat, its Kangaroo, its farming, its prints and
  flowers* (London, King and Tarett, 1923)
Simpson, A. W.: *The Australian Tour* (Brighton, Brighton Herald, 1953)
Statham, Brian:
  Cricket Merry-go-round (London, Stanley Paul, 1956)
  Spell at the Top (London, Souvenir Press, 1969)
Swanton, E. W.:
  Elusive Victory (London, Hodder & Stoughton, 1951)
  The Test Matches of 1953 (London, Daily Telegraph, 1953)
  The Test Matches of 1954–55 (London, Daily Telegraph, 1955)
  The Test Matches of 1956 (London, Daily Telegraph, 1956)
  Cricket from All Angles (London, Michael Joseph, 1968)
Thompson, A. A.: *Cricketers of My Times* (London, Stanley Paul, 1967)

Times Cricket Correspondent:
  The Story of the Test Matches in 1950–51 (London, The Times, 1951)
  The Ashes 1956 (London, The Times, 1956)
Warner, Sir Pelham: *Long Innings* (London, Harrap, 1951)
Warner, Rex and Blair, Lyle: *Ashes to Ashes* (London, MacGibbon & Kee, 1951)
Washbrook, Cyril: *Cricket – the Silver Lining* (London, Sportsguide, 1950)
Wellings, E. M.:
  No Ashes for England (London, Evans, 1951)
  Meet the Australians (London, Evening News, 1953)
  The Ashes Retained (London, Evans, 1955)
West, Peter (Editor):
  Cricketers from Australia (London, Playfair, 1953)
  The Fight for the Ashes 1953 (London, Harrap, 1953)
Whitington, R. S.: (See also under Miller, Keith and Whitington, R.S.)
  Fours Galore (London, Cassell, 1969)
  Simpson's Safari (London, Heinemann, 1967)
  The Quiet Australian (London, Heinemann, 1969)
  An Illustrated History of Australian Cricket (London, Pelham Books, 1974)
White, Crawford:
  The England Victory 1953 (London, News Chronicle, 1953)
  England Keep the Ashes (London, News Chronicle, 1955)
  The Ashes Retained 1956 (London, News Chronicle, 1956)
Yardley, Norman: *Cricket Campaigns* (London, Stanley Paul, 1950)

NEWSPAPERS AND PERIODICALS

Daily Express
Daily Graphic
Daily Herald
Daily Mail
Daily Sketch
Daily Telegraph
Evening News
Evening Standard
Morning Advertiser
News Chronicle
News of the World
The Observer
The People
Star
Sunday Express
Sunday Sun, Sydney
Sydney Daily Telegraph
The Cricketer
The Times
Unicorn, Melbourne High School Magazine, 1934–36
Victorian Cricket Association Annual Report for the seaons 1938–39, 1945–46,
    1946–47 and 1947–48
Western Mail
Wisden
Yorkshire Post

Index